A SURVIVORS'
HAGGADAH

PASSOVER SERVICE

MUNICH ENCLAVE

Munich, Germany, April 15-16, 1946

A SURVIVORS'
HAGGADAH

WRITTEN, DESIGNED, AND ILLUSTRATED BY
YOSEF DOV SHEINSON WITH WOODCUTS BY
MIKLÓS ADLER, BOTH HAVING BEEN AMONG
THE *SHE'ERITH HAPLETAH*, THE REMNANT
THAT ESCAPED. ORIGINALLY PUBLISHED IN
MUNICH 1946 FOR THE FIRST PASSOVER AFTER
LIBERATION AND PRINTED BY THE US ARMY OF
OCCUPATION, HERE PRESENTED IN A FACSIM-
ILE EDITION WITH AN ENGLISH TRANSLATION.

**Edited with an introduction and commentary
by Saul Touster**

JEWISH PUBLICATION SOCIETY
PHILADELPHIA 2000/5760

Jewish Publication Society
2100 Arch Street
Philadelphia, PA 19103

First published in 1998 as a limited edition by
The American Jewish Historical Society.
This edition has been revised.

Book design, typography, and production by
Scott-Martin Kosofsky
at the Philidor Company, Cambridge.

99 00 01 02 03 04 05 06 07 08   10 9 8 7 6 5 4 3 2 1

Library of Congress Cataloging-in-Publication Data:

Haggadah (Sheynzon).   Polyglot.
      A survivors' Haggadah / written, designed and illustrated by
Yosef Dov Sheinson ; with woodcuts by Miklós Adler ; edited and with
an introduction by Saul Touster.
            p.   cm.
      Contains original Hebrew and Yiddish text with English
translation.
      "Originally published in Munich 1946 for the first Passover after
liberation and printed by the US Army of Occupation. Here presented
in a facsimile edition with an English translation."
      Includes bibliographical references.
      ISBN: 0–8276–0686–9
      1. Haggadot Texts.   2. Seder—Liturgy Texts.   3. Judaism—Liturgy
Texts.   4. Haggadah (Sheynzon)   I. Sheynzon, Y. D. (Yosef Dov),
1907–1990. II. Touster, Saul. III. Title.
BM674.75.S54   1999
296.4'5371—dc21   99–37142
                                                                              CIP

Printed in the United States of America

This edition is dedicated to
the *She'erith Hapletah*, those who survived,
and among them the maker of this Haggadah
Y. D. Sheinson
and the woodcut artist
Miklós Adler.

IN MEMORY

ACKNOWLEDGMENTS

IN THE WORK undertaken here, I have tried to recover and memorialize the making of a Haggadah that is full of both the terrible flames of the Holocaust and the seed that escaped and sprang in green stock from its ashes. As a researcher and editor with little Hebrew or Yiddish, I have had to rely at every hand on the patience and generosity of strangers and friends. In many instances, the strangers became friends—which may be the mark of an inquiry into a subject so involved with deep feelings and the trials of memory. To thank them here is hardly adequate unless I consider that we were all part of the work of remembrance. For the translators, their help has been more than a translation, it has been an education for me. For the witnesses of events, I thank them for their openness of heart and mind. For the keepers of history, at universities, libraries, and archives, I thank them not just for their patience and courtesy, but for the hints and leads they gave me through the difficult terrain of unfamiliar languages. I thank my colleagues at Brandeis University and its Judaica Library for their continuous encouragement and sustenance. All of these, who were so important to this work, I should like to thank by name.

Rabbi Abraham J. Klausner, intrepid chaplain to the *She'erith Hapletah*, gave essential help through advice and recollection. The generous help of Mrs. Liza Sheinson of Montreal, the widow of Y. D. Sheinson, the maker of this Haggadah, was crucial to my telling of the Sheinson story. The late John Najmann of London, a survivor and witness to some of these events, whose strong interest in the "A" Haggadah animated my work, became my friend. Sadly, he died in Israel on a mission to Yad Vashem—to establish a fund for the work of remembrance—before this edition was completed. His brother

Herbert Najmann of Israel has carried on in John's spirit. Among the family of the woodcut artist Miklós Adler, who came through the Holocaust as he did, were several who helped me. Adler's sister, Mrs. Eva Adler Klein of London, shared with me his painful story as well as his art work and personal photos, much enriching my understanding. The others—Adler's nephew, Gabor Katz, of Staten Island, N.Y.; his sister-in-law, Mrs. Irene Katz, of Brooklyn; and his close friend, Yoel Horovitz, of Holon, Israel—all contributed their memories. Special thanks must be given to Tirza Oren, researcher at the Yad Vashem Historical Museum. She was critical to my discovery of who the true artist of the woodcuts was, and a great help with materials at Yad Vashem. Shlomo Shafir, a survivor who knew Sheinson well, contributed details about Sheinson and the publishing of the Sheinson Haggadah, the predecessor edition to the "A" Haggadah. The children of Joe Levine—Stanley Levine of Fort Wayne, Indiana, and Lois L. Edwards of Chicago—were generous in recounting Joe's life story. Lucian K. Truscott IV, grandson of General Truscott who was governor general of Bavaria when the Haggadah was made, provided a valuable perspective on his grandfather's character. Dr. Juliane Wetzel of the Technische Universität Berlin, Zentrum für Antisemitismusforschung, a specialist on Jewish life in Munich after the war, was helpful with documentation.

The translators require special mention. Yaron Peleg brought a deep sense of the rhetoric of Hebrew and a breadth of biblical allusion. My Yiddish translators, both survivors and DPs who lived near Munich at the time of the making of the Haggadah—Robert Szulkin at Landsberg and Rabbi Marc Samuels at Feldafing—gave me vivid reminders of that world.

In my library research, I relied on Dr. Charles Cutter, the Brandeis Judaica librarian and university archivist, and his assistant, James Rosenbloom, for their generous day-to-day help as translators and reference guides. Also helpful were Dr. Zachary M. Baker, head librarian, YIVO Institute for Jewish Research; Ronald Finegold, reference librarian, Montreal Jewish Public Library; Dr. Michael Ryan, director of special collections, University of Pennsylvania Library, and Dr. Sol Cohen, researcher at its Center for Judaic

Studies; Dr. Pearl Berger, librarian, Yeshiva University Library; and Dr. Kathryn A. Jacob and others at the American Jewish Historical Society.

Continuous help and encouragement came from Brandeis colleagues whom I thank: foremost, Robert Szulkin and Sylvia Fuks-Fried; Leon Jick, Tsvi Abusch, Antony Polonsky, and Jonathan Sarna of the Department of Near Eastern and Judaic Studies; Thomas Doherty in my own Department of American Studies; Edward Kaplan; Vera Deak, of the library, who translated the Hungarian for me; university photographer Julian Brown; and President Jehuda Reinharz, a distinguished scholar in modern Jewish history.

I wish to give my thanks to Yehuda Bauer, exemplary scholar in the field of Holocaust and survivor studies; and to historians Gerd Korman, Randolph L. Braham, and Alex Grobman. I also thank John Felstiner, scholar-translator at Stanford; Theodore Feder of JDC, in Munich from 1945 through the DP period; Aviram Paz, collector of Haggadot, of Kibbutz Mishmar Ha'emek, Israel, who was (for me) the first discoverer of Adler's *Fametszete*; Dr. Shalom Eilati of Israel, son of Israel Kaplan; and *Histachdut Oley Hungaria*, the Hungarian immigrant organization in Israel.

From the time I first envisioned this project, Michael Feldberg recognized its importance and its connection to American Jewry. As executive director of the American Jewish Historical Society, he worked as proponent and guiding spirit in bringing out this book, while giving me generous personal support. Scott-Martin Kosofsky, responsible for book design, typography, and production, brought his creative energies not only to the making of the book but to subtle matters of content and language. It was a pleasure working with him.

The final words of thanks are for my wife, Irene Tayler. Her personal support, her scholarly and stylistic good sense, her fine taste, her daily help—both spiritual and practical—all accompanied me on the journey of remembrance that this work has been.

—*S. T.*

INTRODUCTION*

IN NINETEEN NINETY-SIX, during the week before Passover, having sold our house I was engaged in the heavy business of going through the photos, papers, and memorabilia of four generations when the Haggadah reprinted here fell from one of my father's files. My reactions as I looked through its pages shifted from curiosity on seeing the bright "A" of the military emblem on the cover to surprise at the Haggadah's place and date—Munich, April 15–16, 1946—to a stunned fascination as I took in its visual details. More from instinct than any informed knowledge, I knew that the art work here, both the woodcuts and the border designs vividly associating the Passover story of the Exodus with the liberation from Nazi horror, had been created by survivors of the Holocaust. In the spring of 1946, few people in the general public, or even informed Jews, knew in such detail the process and places of extermination. This Haggadah had been made by people with first-hand knowledge.

The most immediate personal questions for me concerned the undated handwritten inscription on the inside of the cover: *To Mr. and Mrs. Touster as a reminder that they and others made it possible for our people to leave Germany and live as free men and women in Israel.* Signed: *Joe Levine.* Who was Joe

---

* Composite notes to this introduction, with references, biographical accounts, and comments, appear at the end of the book, by the page. Abbreviations used here are: UNRRA (United Nations Relief and Rehabilitation Agency), the official agency administering aid to DPs (Displaced Persons); and JDC (American Jewish Joint Distribution Committee) which, under the authority of UNRRA, the Occupation, or other governments, provided aid for Jews.

Levine? Why had he made this inscription to my parents—American-born, long residents of New York, never near Europe during the war years, certainly not in 1946? Of course, the mention of Israel meant that the inscription was written *after* the founding of Israel in 1948. Slowly it dawned: it concerned my family that had long been involved in HIAS, the Hebrew Immigrant Aid Society. Indeed, as a young man I had served as its assistant general counsel. My father had served as its president in the early 1950s, and so it was probable that he received the Haggadah in that capacity, perhaps on a trip to the refugee camps of Europe. That he kept this among his personal things suggested it was special for him, as it surely has become for me. I determined to learn everything I could about this Haggadah—a rare one, as I later learned.

The process—of search and research—was in one sense odd. I knew little Hebrew or Yiddish, and as a scholar in law and American Studies I knew enough to be wary of swimming in unfamiliar waters. Nonetheless this was a call I could not turn away from, and with the encouragement and help of colleagues at Brandeis University, specialists in various aspects of Judaica, I undertook to explore to the fullest this Haggadah that so clearly reflected not only on the Holocaust, but on the American relation to it.

Created by survivors and used for the celebration of the first Passover after the liberation of the camps and the Allied victory over Nazi Germany, this edition of this Haggadah was printed early in 1946 by the U.S. Army of Occupation, the Third Army whose "A" insignia the cover bears. The Haggadah was thus among the first published in Germany after the Nazi regime. The Seders that the Haggadah announces were conducted by an army chaplain, Rabbi Abraham J. Klausner, who was at the time prominent for his work among the survivors of Dachau and his care of the *She'erith Hapletah*, the Saved Remnant, 'the few who escaped.' Most of the celebrants at the Seders—sitting among representatives of the Allied forces, military government, and civilian aid people—were these survivors. To have a Seder of two hundred in a public facility in the heart of Munich in 1946 was a signal event. But to appreciate fully the Haggadah and the Seders, we must look to their historic setting.

Historic Background

One might think that the Holocaust ended when the concentration camps were liberated and the Germans capitulated on May 8, 1945. But that is not the case. In the months before the end, the Germans had driven thousands of prisoners on forced marches from the eastern death camps to the west, partly in the last hope of providing slave laborers for their factories, partly as a killing method. In most cases only a few of the marchers survived, and many of these few were dying as the war ended. In the concentration camps, for weeks after liberation, starvation and disease and death were rampant, even after a sustaining diet was introduced and medical attention given. And for those who survived those dark post-liberation weeks, conditions did not change enough to speak of real liberation. Many of the survivors were still confined in the camps, often behind barbed wire, guarded now by Allied soldiers under conditions of continued deprivation. Of the tens of millions of European DPs, the surviving Jews were a very small number and were thrown together in the DP camps with non-Jewish DPs of an entirely different kind, many of whom were often vehemently anti-Semitic. There were large numbers of them from the Baltics, the Ukraine, and elsewhere who had volunteered to work in German factories and fields—people reasonably well fed and never imprisoned or tortured. There were those who had collaborated in the east and had been driven west by Soviet advances, now homeless and fearful of returning home. There were even numbers of Soviet deserters, or prisoners of war, who had formed several active units fighting for the German army. There were Polish DPs who may themselves have been in the Nazi camps or driven from their homes by one army or the next. Finally, there were the German civilian DPs themselves, some returning home from conquered territories, some ethnic Germans driven from countries where they had been long settled. As for Jews who had, on their own, headed home to Poland or the Ukraine, they met with anti-Semitic hostility and violence and were refused their property. Some of this violence (winked at or supported by the new governments and eventually leading to full-scale pogroms) drove these Jews, too, back to the DP camps in the west. This unfolding drama, a kind of last act of the Holocaust, played out against a background of Allied policies which, no matter how well intended, could be viewed as a continuation of persecution of the Jews.

Those early established policies were fivefold: (1) to carry out repatriation without exception (i.e., Polish Jews to Poland, or German Jews apparently to stay on in Germany); (2) to establish or maintain DP camps by nationality alone, thus including Ukrainian Jews with, for example, Ukrainians who had volunteered to work for the Nazis; (3) to maintain equality in the treatment of DPs, treating half-starved Jewish slave laborers, held in captivity for years, equally (even as to calories) with late-arriving healthy laborers who may have volunteered for German service; (4) to consider Jews who had German or other Axis nationality as 'enemy nationals'; and (5) to restore the DPs' physical and mental condition to where they could become productive workers in the recovery of Europe's economy. Even though physical conditions in the camps eased as the months went on, these policies created an impossible world for the Jews. By then, knowing of conditions in Eastern Europe, the Jews resisted repatriation and insisted on being recognized as 'stateless persons.' The 'equal' treatment that was provided was a bureaucratic delusion. And as for working to restore the German economy, Jews wanted no part of it. The theory of repatriation soon became a choking point for those who couldn't go home and couldn't go elsewhere, not to Palestine, nor as immigrants to the United States, or Canada, or South America. They were in effect trapped and their despair echoed in the cry, "We were liberated, but we are not free."

By late spring of 1945 this irrational and cruel system began to falter as press reports of scandalous conditions under which the survivors were kept brought worldwide protest. American army Jewish chaplains, as well as other chaplains, brought dramatic attention within the military and outside to the untenable policies and conditions. The American Jewish community marshaled its political resources to bring pressure for a change if not of heart, at least of policy. Jewish agencies, frustrated in their giving aid, added to the pressure. News stories of Jewish DPs being placed in camps under confinement among former collaborator guards and tormentors were making the Occupation look immoral and ridiculous. Within the Truman administration, strong representations were made for changes in policy, both in treating the DPs and opening up immigration to Palestine. The British continued to resist. With strong backing from Secretary of Treasury Henry Morgenthau and with General Eisenhower's acquiescence, the Sate Department began a process of inquiry in June. After an initial rebuff from President Truman, it persuaded him to appoint a commission headed by Earl G. Harrison, dean of the University of Pennsylvania Law School, with a mandate to investigate and report on the condition of the DPs, especially as related to the Jews. The commission worked expeditiously, and within seven weeks preliminary conclusions regarding shameful conditions in the treatment of the Jews were cabled by the War Department to European headquarters and a process of change began. The final Harrison Report that was issued in September was highly critical, with detailed descriptions that supported this astonishing conclusion: "As matters now stand, we appear to be treating the Jews as the Nazis treated them except that we do not exterminate them."

This extreme judgment would be sustained, despite the army's acknowledgedly positive performance in the overall movement and care of millions of DPs. Eisenhower's response was to make major changes of policy and practice. He appointed Army Chaplain Judah Nadich as special advisor on Jewish affairs to function at headquarters level with direct access to him. Nadich was not only to consult on policy but to serve as liaison with Jewish aid agencies and as a clearinghouse of complaints. Nadich soon uncovered a number of standing orders already in place which, if carried out as they should have been, would have alleviated some of the problems pointed out by the Harrison Commission. Eisenhower issued orders to enforce those policies and to change others. It was then that the Jews were officially separated into all-Jewish camps and hospitals and given the special care they needed. As to diet, the Jews were given 200 calories in addition to the standard 2,000 calories a day, though this was sometimes more a goal than a reality. Jews who returned from Eastern Europe were to be received into the DP camps and given aid. Eisenhower acted forcefully and dramatically in firing General Patton, who had been the responsible commander in the Army of Occupation in Southern

Germany. Earlier, Eisenhower had to order Patton to change his practice of keeping the Jews confined to camp under armed guard and he had to countermand Patton's refusal to admit into DP camps Polish Jews who came back from Poland. In addition, it became clear that Patton had disobeyed or failed to carry out standing orders with respect to denazification policy and directives that German properties such as housing and food be requisitioned and given to Nazi victims. Patton's fraternization with the German elite could only have made matters worse. The new commander of the Third Army, Gen. Lucian K. Truscott, also a battle-hardened soldier, was a more patient and sympathetic military governor than Patton and capable of dealing with political and moral complexity. The Eisenhower-mandated changes of policy and command effected substantial improvement in the conditions of the Jewish DPs. One could see an emerging good sense and even humanitarian spirit in the military command, especially in the examples of Eisenhower and Truscott.

Even though the number of Jewish DPs was a small fraction of the DP population, the seemingly intractable problem of their future became preoccupying for both the army and the Allied governments. With the Jews not being repatriated, with Palestine blockaded against their entry, and emigration to America and elsewhere practically barred to them, the army's problems were exacerbated by a steady flow of Jews, at first spontaneous and then highly organized, from Eastern Europe into the American zones. The hostility toward Jews in Poland and the Ukraine had increased rather than moderated as time went on. Any thought of remaining there, under Soviet domination, became untenable. In August 1945 there had been about 50,000 Jews in Germany and Austria. Their numbers grew continually, with the flow from the east turning into a flood after the pogrom in Kielce, Poland, in July 1946. That flood would be identified as the *Brichah* ('the flight'), led at first by Jewish underground leaders but soon taken over by Palestinian emissaries, *shlihim*. Although mainly illegal in operation, the *Brichah* sometimes had the tacit or open support of local governments and UNRRA. Over time, some local authorities were more and more cooperative, especially when UNRRA or JDC footed the bills for care and transportation, and then there would be a 'winking' that was equivalent to a license for transit through a country as more Jews headed west. As for the sometimes reluctant American military, they were resigned to receiving all who would come. Thus, over a period of the three years 1945 through 1948 the *Brichah* would bring some 250,000 displaced Jews into the American zones. Many tried illegal entry into Palestine—*Brichah's* eventual destination—but most stayed in the DP camps for the time being, trapped and waiting.

The Government of the Jews: Toward the First Passover

The Jewish survivors of the Holocaust, the most special of victims, had become the most difficult of wards. And yet from those first terrible weeks after liberation, and before a year had passed, the Jews moved slowly and effectively toward self-government and the creation of a vital though wounded community. The first rescuers of their bodies were, of course, the Allied armies and their medical corps—from the Russian soldiers entering Auschwitz in January 1945 to the American soldiers entering Dachau late in April. But the balm to their spirit, at least in the west, were the army chaplains. The first task was to bury the dead in decent and sacred burial. This was the work of the chaplains. The next task was to find who had survived, for without that knowledge no husband could find wife, no mother her children, no family be reunited. This task, too, was aided by the chaplains. In this immediate caring response the chaplains earned a lasting memory among the *She'erith Hapletah*, the surviving remnant. To focus on the Munich area, which was at the center of survivors in Germany, is to bring to our attention the U.S. Army chaplain Rabbi Abraham J. Klausner, who played a key role in the printing and use of the Haggadah reproduced here.

A brief outline of Klausner's work tells us much about the story of self-government and industry among the Jews. Within weeks of the liberation at Dachau, after the bodies found piled up or strewn about the camp had been buried as decently (ritually) as possible in mass graves and the new dead were being given individual burials, the survivors with the help of Klausner began the project of listing those who had survived. With this as the basis of a tracing bureau, a newborn organization identified as the Central Committee of Liberated Jews of Bavaria published with the help of Klausner a first volume of lists under the title *Sharit Ha-Platah*, and it published four more volumes by January 1946. According to the historian Yehuda Bauer, this was the first time in a published source in Germany that the term was used to designate the saved remnant of survivors.

In an economy of extreme scarcity, with paper and printing facilities tightly controlled, and within the complex and often irrational regulatory system of the Occupation, the five volumes were printed through Klausner's intrepid and resourceful 'organizing.' He reports how he found a small back-street German printer who printed the first four volumes in exchange for coffee and the paper supplies taken from Dachau (where a paper mill had been functioning). When Klausner eventually persuaded the army how important family tracing was for the morale and recovery of the Jewish DPs, the army itself printed the fifth volume. In similar fashion, Klausner's efforts to help the Central Committee to represent the survivors in negotiations with Occupation authorities reflected not only his 'organizing' powers, but also tendencies in the army to wink sympathetically at technical violations. For example, in late June 1945, after lower echelon command had accepted Klausner's efforts at survivor organization, a higher echelon intervened and a colonel called Klausner to account. Klausner describes the meeting:

> [The colonel] understood that I wanted to organize. . . . But, he
> said, unfortunately we cannot permit you to proceed. . . . I could
> not set up this organization . . . he explained this was a ruling of
> the Army . . . [A]s I walked to the door, and my back was towards
> him, he said to me: 'but do a good job.' So I smiled, thanked him
> again, and walked out. . . . And we were in business.

After this interview, Klausner picked up a truckload of 'organized' lumber out of Dachau stores and drove to the largely bombed-out Deutsches Museum in Munich to have the Central Committee's offices built in space he had previously secured from UNRRA. The furniture was no doubt 'liberated,' as were the materials he later provided to shelter at the museum a large group of Jewish DPs who had resisted repatriation.

Just as Klausner worked for acceptance of the Central Committee, he helped the Committee in its founding of its Yiddish weekly, *Unzer Weg* (Our Way). Levi Shalit, a Lithuanian survivor, a newsman working with the Committee, approached Klausner with the idea, and from there events unfolded expeditiously as the historian Alex Grobman recounts them:

> The first priority was to find Hebrew type, so Klausner arranged for Shalit to visit Frankfurt where, in the Stempel Publishing House, Shalit found type that had been used in printing prayer books before the war. [Eisenhower's special advisor] Judah Nadich obtained permission for him to take the type to Munich, [Chaplain] Max Braude [of the Seventh Army, headquartered in Heidelberg] secured the authorization to have new type cast, and Klausner provided paper from the Dachau warehouse.

In the saga of the American army chaplains who responded quickly and with extraordinary devotion on behalf of the survivors, often at the risk of court-martial, Klausner stands out for his commitment to one transforming idea: the self-governance of the survivors. Marshaling against one bureaucracy or another—that of the military government preoccupied with security, or of UNRRA, deeply reflecting international politics, or of JDC, heavily dependent upon government authority—Klausner was moved by his conviction that self-government was the key to overcoming the malaise of despair among the survivors, restoring their dignity and releasing their energies. Today we might think of this as obvious. But in 1945, in a world that had turned humans into things, when even caring was laced with the patron's condescension, this idea was radical and upsetting. One can see why *Unzer Weg* should write of Klausner in its first editorial—"And so it came that he was called the first American member of the *She'erith Hapletah*."

At this point one cannot help but go back and address the moral aspect of

Klausner's 'organizing' and, indeed, *Brichah's* 'illegality.' For the surviving Jews at this time, Europe was still fouled by the moral collapse that was the Holocaust. That collapse was not anarchy but a system—murderous and irrational as it might be—a well-organized system, heavily bureaucratized and hierarchical, recording its activities in every detail and forcing its victim to partake of the system. Imagine then the survivor's rescue as he faces—what? Another system, albeit one with good intentions. And in this system were three overlapping bureaucracies: a military one, highly hierarchical and detail driven; a civil one in a military government slowly becoming civilian; and an aid system moved by a desire to do the right thing for the objects of its bounty. In the care of such bureaucracies, dealt with as objects, the survivors would aspire only to be persons and perforce treat the system as they were treated by it. They use or abuse the system, they evade it, they manipulate it, or they charm it. That is, to preserve their lives and protect their meager goods they 'organize' things within and against the system. Is it any wonder, then, that the term 'organize' would run through the armies and prisons of the world just as it ran in the many languages of captivity through the concentration camp (*lager*) system? As one who escaped Treblinka and survived Auschwitz put it:

> —*organizing* was probably the most important word in the Lager's vocabulary. I soon learned that organizing meant getting; and doing; and making some one else do it; but most of all, it meant stealing without being caught. Because if you were caught stealing, then you were a thief, and as a thief you would be severely punished. As an organizer you were respected.

This survivor's thoughts were aroused by the recollection of an old prisoner's handing out shoes to new slave laborers. The shoes "were made of hard, stiff sheepskin, and had heavy wooden soles. They had no shoestrings and were much too large. . . . He said the shoes would move as we walked, and that our feet would get ulcers unless we 'organized' shoestrings." *Shoestrings!*— obviously matters of life and death. The 'organizing' and 'illegality' we see throughout the DP period were, for the Jews, responses of necessity in an amoral world and a small advance on control over their own lives.

During the months after the Central Committee was legitimized as the organ of self-government, the Jews experienced great changes. By April, under the auspices of UNRRA, the Committee—democratically elected and composed of a group of distinguished and capable leaders—was pretty much running the camps, from policy making to the exercise of everyday police powers. The army, recognizing the DPs' needs in religion, culture, and education, had begun to give substantial support for Hebrew religious texts, for Yiddish newspapers, and cultural and educational activities. *Unzer Weg* with army support published its first issue on October 12, 1945; six months later, on April 15, 1946, the day of Passover eve, it would publish its 28th issue, carrying sixteen pages of international, regional, local, and personal news. As described by Leo Schwarz, a senior JDC official in Germany and later the first historian of the period, *Unzer Weg* was received "in the editorial offices in Paris, London, New York, Tel Aviv, Vienna . . . a mine of information to the news-hungry editors." He concluded that "this paper out of the ruins of Munich was proof of vitality and of a faint glimmering of cultural renascence."

The Passover eve issue was, as would be expected, full of the Passover theme and the bittersweetness of the Exodus from Egypt echoing in the hope of an Exodus from Europe. The editor, Levi Shalit, in its lead article, spoke out with that double voice. *Today is Passover, the spring holiday of our people as a nation. . . . And one wants so much, dear sister and brother Jews who survived the catastrophe, to hear at least today a word of consolation—today, at the first liberated Passover, after six years of bloody Sabbaths and holidays, today, on the happiest day of our people.* In this spirit of consolation Shalit advises against personal memory. *Don't tell that your children were gassed in chambers. . . . Don't tell how you slaved . . . don't draw a parallel between Hitler and Pharaoh, but instead let us read the ancient Haggadah which always renewed us in the Diaspora. . . .* But even as he advises against the pain of drawing that parallel, he invokes its power for hope. *Tell it on the last night of the Seder, here, in the European desert, on your way to your liberation.*

There are other items concerning Passover—"Erev Pesach in Munich" full of "bitter herbs and little enough matzah"; another item drawing the parallels between Exodus and the Holocaust, between Pharaoh and Hitler; another about a modernized Haggadah with such questions as, "Why do we have to rebuild Europe?"; and still another that echoed 'Pour out your wrath upon the nations.' Beside all of these was the full array of international news, Palestine news, local news of the camps, a Sholem Aleichem story, a report on the Nuremberg trial, another on the Dachau trials, a memoir from the Warsaw Ghetto, notices, personals. In at least one article we hear of the meeting of the United Zionist Organization for the Saved Remnant in Germany (*Achida*) and its urgings for unity among the Jews and a lament over political factionalism and splintering.

This last item touches on the sensitive point that, under the conditions of unhealed wounds and rapid social upheaval and change, factionalism would become intense and the splintering bitter, and even the Central Committee was to become politicized by parties. Every faction had a newspaper or newsletter, some regularly printed and some as small as the occasional handwritten issue. Intense competition among survivor groups and parties seethed with the continuations of prewar loyalties and ideologies, religious and secular, Zionist and non-Zionist; and this old politics was now being compounded and intensified by a new politics from within Palestine in its struggles between Left and Right.

The dialogue presented in this Haggadah is itself a dramatic reflection of these conditions. In its text, the emissaries [*shlihim* from Palestine] ask of the surviving remnants: "Which group do you belong to?" The remnants answer: "Are we not, all of us, Israel?" The emissaries say: "You must have been sleeping for seventy years, because the unity of Israel is a fable. It's no longer possible; each person must join a group." The remnants answer: "Was not all of Israel slaughtered together?" The emissaries end with their coda of factions: "Rivalry breeds strength which increases the might of Israel." This certainly satiric exchange appears to reflect the author's position on the hoped-for unity that is advocated by the survivor group *Achida* which, with *Nocham* (United

Pioneer Youth), published the present Haggadah. It is of interest to note that, as organizations, neither had a political prehistory; both came out of the Holocaust, the seeds having been planted in the underground in Kovno, Lithuania. The Lithuanian connections among the Central Committee, *Unzer Weg*, *Achida*, and probably *Nocham* (whose name was not adopted until August 1945), all centered on a unity theme that pervades the Haggadah reproduced here. No unified position was ever achieved, and it's not coincidental that *Achida* and *Nocham* both disappeared along with the Central Committee and *Unzer Weg* after the founding of Israel in 1948 and the coming end of the DP camps.

On Sunday, April 14, 1946, the day before Passover eve, the *New York Times* gave the view from America. Passover matzah was reported to have been baked in Germany for the first time since Nazi power and been distributed by the JDC. In its "News of the Week in Review," the *Times* pictured the international scene: problems of the newly formed United Nations and the appointment of the chair of its Security Council. In its national news: FDR's home at Hyde Park was dedicated as a national shrine, the debate over control of atomic energy continued, and the economic problems concerning the conversion from war to peace persisted. But these domestic concerns did not overshadow the world situation and the problem of "500 million Europeans and Chinese facing starvation." An item, "Refugees Arrive in May," gave the good news-bad news about Europe's survivors: President Truman directed a special admission of between 75,000 and 100,000 "hungry and destitute war casualties," many of whom were guaranteed by a private organization for the care of European children; otherwise immigration would be effectively closed unless Congress acted to change the old quota law. The dimension of the problem was set forth in a piece on "Homeless Europeans" that began as follows:

> At the end of the war there were in Europe about 20,000,000 displaced persons—refugees from political and racial tyranny, slave labor imported to Germany, evacuees fleeing battle areas. Today, all but 1,190,000 DPs have been repatriated. Of those remaining, 900,000 are in DP camps in Germany and Austria—about

450,000 in the American zones, 400,000 in the British zones, 50,000 in the French zones. More than half are Poles; 200,000 are Spanish Republicans exiled in France; the others are chiefly Balts and Jews. Many of the remaining DPs fear to return home because they oppose new regimes, face possible trial as collaborationists if they return, or fear anti-Semitism.

The piece ended with attention to the special plight of the DP Jews who could not be repatriated. Judge Simon Rifkind, the new special advisor on Jewish affairs, reported to the European theater commander, General McNarney (who succeeded Eisenhower): "Rapid mass resettlement is the only means of solving the problem. All of them have but one earnest wish, to be quit of Europe; and most of them have one other compelling desire, to emigrate to Palestine.... I believe their problem is actually insoluble without Palestine."

The First Passover: The "A" Haggadah

When the first Passover came, large numbers of Jews of the *She'erith Hapletah* gathered in the Munich area to celebrate in Seders of every variety from Kosher Orthodox traditional to non-Orthodox and nontraditional. There were large Seders, such as those at the main Jewish camps at Landsberg, Feldafing, Foehrenwald, and the hospital at St. Ottilien, and smaller ones at lesser camps or places of assembly, and some in the city itself. Among the latter were Seders held in the Deutsches Theater Restaurant for two hundred DPs living in Munich outside the camps—at this time there were some 6,000 of them—together with representatives of the Allied forces and civilian aid people. As announced by the "A" Haggadah, these Seders were conducted by Chaplain Klausner. For all of Germany's Seders, the matzah was provided in large measure by JDC's newly reestablished bakeries in Germany and supplemented by imports. The food and wine were provided by the established sources: UNRRA, the Army of Occupation, or JDC.

It's unclear what Haggadot were used at most of these various Seders. Abraham Yaari in the introduction to his great *Bibliography of the Passover*

Haggadah (1960) notes: "These [Haggadah] editions were printed in Israel, England and the United States, and sent to the [DP]camps through various charitable institutions. Some editions were printed by the inmates of the camps themselves in Germany and Holland, and to these were added special chapters on the recent events and the conclusions to be drawn from them." Among the Haggadot created by survivors themselves for this first Passover, the most finished in its extraordinary decorations and woodcuts, and the most comprehensive in paralleling Exodus and Holocaust, was this Haggadah first published by *Achida* and *Nocham*, later to become the "A" Haggadah. Although self-described as a "Supplement" to the Haggadah, it was and is acknowledged as a Haggadah and included among the standard bibliographies and commentaries as one of the few Haggadot that were created by survivors for the first Passover after the war. Despite the involved history of publication, printing, and reprinting of this Haggadah, the heart of the work was done not by a group or organization but by one dedicated man, himself a survivor of four years of Nazi camps—Yosef Dov Sheinson. He wrote, arranged, designed, decorated, and edited the Haggadah and chose the powerful woodcuts done by another survivor. On the title page his initials appear at the lower left of the design and the caption below: *Arranged and illustrated by Y. D. Sheinson.* Although others surely helped him produce the finished booklet, this might be called the Sheinson Haggadah.

Although time has clouded some details of the publishing history, the main features and origins of the Sheinson Haggadah that became the "A" Haggadah seem clear from an account by Shlomo Shafir, the then director of education and cultural activities of *Achida* in Munich. By November 1945, *Achida* had secured Hebrew and Yiddish type through American Jewish organizations for its periodicals just at the time that Sheinson was composing his Haggadah. Early in 1946, after Sheinson had written, drawn, made up the Haggadah, and incorporated into it the seven woodcuts, Shafir brought the paste-up pages to a major Munich publishing house, Bruckmann, K.G. In exchange for cigarettes and UNRRA food, Bruckmann photo-engraved zinc plates and printed by letterpress the edition of the Sheinson Haggadah—a not unusual transaction in those days when cigarettes and food were forms of currency. Shafir ironically observed that Bruckmann's owners, prominent before the war, had been "vehement supporters of Adolf Hitler and introduced him in the 1920's to Munich's high society." The house was also said to have printed other Zionist materials for *Achida* and other groups. Whether Bruckmann facilities had by then been taken by the military government and given over to non-Nazi publishers is not now known. (See my commentary on page 2 of the text ahead.) In any case, very soon after this first publication two editors from *Unzer Weg*, Levi Shalit and Israel Kaplan, took the Haggadah to Klausner, suggesting that it be used for a Seder. Klausner decided that the Seder be held in Munich for those living outside the camps as well as for representatives of Allied army units, civilian government, and aid agencies; and that the Haggadah, with a new preface in English, be reprinted on good stock through army press facilities. Thus, with a new cover emblazoned with the tricolor insignia "A" for the Third Army (the Army of Occupation in Bavaria), and an additional English title page and epigraph, as well as Klausner's two-page introduction in English, the Sheinson Haggadah took on another life with its emblematic "A."

But the publishing history does not do justice to the making of the Haggadah by Sheinson and the artist of the woodcuts. Sheinson's life story is a compelling one. In 1940 when the Soviets took over Lithuania under the Hitler-Stalin Pact, Sheinson was thirty-three years old. He had attended medical school in Kovno before turning to education and establishing his name as a teacher and writer in modern Hebrew. A strong Zionist, he had obtained an immigration certificate to Palestine before the Soviet takeover, but the circumstances foreclosed its use. At the German invasion of June 22, 1941, he was among the Jews in Lithuania who were caught in the Nazi killing machine. A vigorous athletic man who had been a leader in the Maccabees, he survived three years in the ghetto of Šiauliai (Shavli), the largest city in northwestern Lithuania, from where Jews were detailed for heavy labor in construction, mines, quarries, and factory sites. In 1943 the ghetto was transformed into a concentration camp, and while many of the Jews there were being taken to the death camps, in 1944 Sheinson was selected along with others capable of heavy labor to be transported to Dachau-Kaufering, near Landsberg, not far from Munich. Kaufering was one of the slave-labor camps within the Dachau complex that were devoted to construction of underground factories. Here he labored until he was selected as one of 800 men transported to Czechoslovakia for work on road construction. Of these 800, Sheinson was one of eighty who survived, until he was liberated by the Soviet army in late April 1945. By this time down to eighty pounds, he was placed in the Theresienstadt camp after its liberation. But he decided, in the words of his widow, "to take his life into his own hands." Crawling under the barbed wire fence, he left the camp, wandered barefoot, was helped by a farmer, and then collapsed to wake up in a hospital where he received good care. After recovery, he was sent to Prague to a Jewish community rest home. By now committed to moving west into the American zone, during that summer he was led by the *Brichah* to the large DP camp at Landsberg administered by American authorities.

Here at Landsberg he renewed friendships from among the Kovno Zionist group that was then organizing and growing in the DP camps as the United Zionist Organization, the *Achida*. Soon he moved into a private home with other survivors in Munich and began work as a teacher in a newly organized Hebrew School, a writer for *Dos Wort* (The Word), the Yiddish paper of *Achida*, and contributing editor to the Hebrew journal *Nitzotz* (The Spark). It was then—probably in the winter of 1945—that he produced his Haggadah to be published by *Achida* and *Nocham*, both committed to a Zionist unity platform.

As we can see from the border designs, woodcuts, and Sheinson's texts that interweave with the traditional Haggadah liturgy, two stories unfold: the Passover story of the deliverance from Pharaoh in Egypt and the Holocaust story of the remnant that escaped from Hitler. The Haggadah's epigraph—*We were slaves to Hitler in Germany*—echoes the biblical "We were slaves to Pharaoh in Egypt." And within the eternal reminder of the Passover story to be told again and again is the call here to another remembrance, that of the recent terrible deaths and suffering. Wherever the idea of 'Exodus' appears, it carries not just the ancient story but, more poignantly, the survivors' fixed idea of the necessary exodus from Europe. Despite the fact that Sheinson uses the traditional Haggadah liturgy, he does so selectively, often adapting it or handling it satirically, reflecting an underlying bitterness in the survivor. The bitterness is most explicit in his treatment of the *dayenu*, that hymn of praise to the Lord for his bounteous gifts and favors. Sheinson's rendering is a hymn of reproach, a dark iteration of the disasters and evils that have beset the Jewish people in their current millennium of woes. But bitterness is not the Haggadah's pervading tone. There is in most of it an almost transcendent yearning for a Promised Land, a Zion to be realized not through God's blessings but by the hard work and 'faith' of Zionists. Where the refrain once was 'We would have been content,' the refrain in this *dayenu* seems to cry out to God 'Enough already!' There was no 'deliverance' by God but a 'liberation' by Allied forces. If God can't or won't work miracles, then people must. In narrative and imaginary dialogues, in prayers converted to the survivors' dire circumstance, and in satirical twists, Sheinson uses the forms and style of traditional rabbinic argumentation and invocation to create a latter-day midrash—a faith in the Promised Land without the God who had made the promise.

As Sheinson painfully portrays the splintered life of the *She'erith Hapletah* and the competition among factions for the hearts of the young, one might recall the Israelites in the wilderness described in the Book of Numbers with its factions, controversy, and challenges to the authority of Moses. It is as if the DP period after deliverance from the Holocaust were kin to Israel's wandering in the wilderness after Exodus from Egypt. Thus, at the heart of Sheinson's Haggadah is the call for an end of dissension, for unity among the Jews. In this, Sheinson and the Haggadah bear the same ideology as that of its publishing organizations: unity in Zionism based on the assertion that the one Israel that suffered through the Holocaust is the same one Israel as the *She'erith Hapletah* must be. In this regard, the Yiddish portions and the quotations from Berl Katznelson and David Frischmann, while honoring the vernacular Yiddish, serve to place the Haggadah in the mainstream of both modern Zionist thought (Katznelson) and the revival of Hebrew as a language and literature (Frischmann). As for speaking of or to God in 1946: in the face of all that has happened, Sheinson is silent.

Overall, the Haggadah is most impressive in its composition, especially Sheinson's hand-drawn title and colophon pages and border designs that carry the text forward page after page. His designs, simple as they are, are rich and suggestive in an iconography that juxtaposes the stories of Exodus and Holocaust and places both of them against a background of the natural world (Eden before the fall) and the Promised Land (the world redeemed). The border decorations, replete with their flowers and trees, their fruits of the soil, their flowing streams, display a world of a lost paradise in the past and a future land of milk and honey. In their starkly different style, the seven harrowing woodcuts of scenes from within the killing camps come as stunning reminders of the fallen world, augmenting the power of the central theme. It should be noted that the captions beneath six of the seven woodcuts carry lines introduced by Sheinson from the traditional Haggadah, as if this invocation from the roots of Exodus was directed at the Holocaust itself. The seventh caption is from the Book of Numbers—*We remember the fish*—referring to the dissension and discontent of Israel in the desert grumbling against God's manna and hungry for flesh. As we learn later, the woodcuts had titles of their own given by the artist, but in the interest of his vision Sheinson moved back mostly to the traditional Passover liturgy or, in one case, to Israel in the wilderness. Designs, text, and woodcuts work together and express a unified vision and politics of one Israel aspiring for the one Zion.

The seven woodcuts do not have signatures or initials in the blocks, but under each woodcut was printed the name *Ben Benyamin*, a name that was first thought to be a pseudonym. When in 1986 a *Jerusalem Post* article commemorated the Sheinson Haggadah on its fortieth anniversary, it carried three of the woodcuts attributing them to "Ben Binyamin [*sic*], whoever he may have been." This 'Ben Benyamin,' this son of the son of the right hand, remained otherwise anonymous until I was already writing this introduction. Until then, all we could deduce about the artist was that he knew the workings of the murderous system he depicted. For me to learn more required months of research until, through the hunch of a persistent researcher at Yad Vashem's Historical Museum and the eye and memory of a collector of Haggadot in Israel, the woodcuts were finally identified as having come from a portfolio of sixteen woodcuts done by a Hungarian artist named Miklós Adler. Although his 'real' name had been hidden from us, it turned out that the name he used was not a pseudonym at all but rather his Hebrew name as the son of his father, Benjamin. The portfolio, depicting sixteen scenes of Holocaust events, had been published in 1945 in Debrecen, Hungary, as sixteen loose sheets of woodcuts placed within a pocket folder, like a large envelope. With no title page, the woodcuts were preceded by five pages of text: an epigraph divided between two pages, as described below; a brief preface appearing on two pages in four languages, Hungarian and Hebrew, English and Russian; and a list of numbered woodcut titles in the same four languages. On the first preface page, the text appeared in parallel columns, one Hungarian and one Hebrew. Beneath the Hungarian column was printed a signature, "*A.M.*," and beneath the Hebrew column a printed signature in Hebrew, "*Ben Benyamin.*" The English and Russian columns on the next page repeated the text but were not signed. The pocket folder's flap served as the colophon, and it alone revealed the identity of "*A.M.*" Inscribed on the flap was "*Adler Miklós/16 Fametszete*" (woodcuts), followed by publishing information in Hungarian, the main part of which was, in translation: "Published/in 1000 numbered copies" by a publisher named 'Freedom' Press ("'*Szabadság' Nyomda*"). Given the conventional name reversal in Hungarian, the artist named 'A.M.' and 'Ben Benyamin' were one and the same: Miklós Adler, Hungarian and Jew.

Miklós Adler, it turned out, was an established Hungarian artist in Debrecen who taught art at the Jewish high school there. He worked in oils and other media including woodcuts from pear wood. After the Nazi takeover of Hungary late in the war, from May to July 1944, 437,000 Hungarian Jews outside of Budapest were transported to Auschwitz. (The Budapest Jews were shut in buildings marked with the Star of David and then in a ghetto from where large numbers were taken in forced marches to heavy-labor sites.) At Auschwitz, some 100,000 were selected for slave labor and the rest killed. One transport, with Adler and his family, was miraculously diverted to Strasshof near Vienna. Or not so miraculously. Apparently the SS, facing a war that was clearly lost, were then in clandestine negotiations for the ransoming of some of the Hungarian Jews. Eichmann's ploy was then "to allow 30,000 Hungarian Jews to be 'put on ice' in Austria." At the same time, it has been suggested, the SS offer was meant to earn credit with the Allies. In any event, the Debrecen transport was diverted and Adler and his family, separated from the awful fate of others, were held 'on ice' in Lager No. 15 in Vienna. If Adler had been sent to Auschwitz he never could have passed 'selection' as he was somewhat lame and an earlier SS beating had left him with serious kidney damage. In spring of 1945, with the Russians approaching Vienna, the prisoners were force-marched for several days and placed in cattle cars to be transported to Theresienstadt, where they were liberated by the Russians on May 8, 1945. It was an irony that Sheinson and Adler should have both been in Theresienstadt during its first days of liberation. Each had been a teacher—Sheinson in Hebrew, Adler in art—who would return to his vocation to teach again in a Hebrew high school. The final irony was that Adler, even after he emigrated to Israel in 1957, never knew of the use of his woodcuts in Sheinson's Haggadah. Whether Sheinson ever saw the flap of the pocket folder that identified 'Ben Benyamin' as Miklós Adler, we cannot say.

On returning to Debrecen Adler made his woodcuts, a kind of chronicle of the Holocaust, and—still in 1945—had them published without a title as described above. (He would later refer to them as "Sufferings in the Concentration Camps.") The woodcuts made their way to Munich by way of DPs who were led by the *Brichah*. Sheinson saw them and chose seven of the sixteen, adding liturgical passages as captions, thus integrating them into the double theme of his Haggadah: Exodus from ancient Egypt and liberation from the Holocaust. In his *16 Fametszete* Adler himself wrote his preface in Hungarian and Hebrew and then had it translated into English and Russian, as if to say that these scenes from the Holocaust were meant to serve as a universal warning to be carried from his own two languages to the world's two great liberating powers in their languages. This monitory reading would seem to be confirmed by the epigraph (also in the four languages) that Adler used, an epigraph he strikingly divided so as to open his work with the words—*Know from where you came,* and at its end close with—*and also know where you are going.* Between these two phrases lie the sixteen woodcuts of Holocaust events. The phrases are well known, appearing in the *Ethics of the Fathers* from which passages are recited in synagogue on Sabbaths after Passover. The final phrase of the quoted passage—words that are here left unspoken—hovers silently over the book: *and before whom you are destined to give a strict accounting.*

I take the words of Adler's personal preface as the epigraph for this present work:

> . . . *one can't find a word to apply to what happened to the Jews of Europe during the past years. Books are going to be written by writers and poets—using documents or experiences—books that will draw for the reader realistic or stylized pictures of what happened. As they unfold, the occurrences will appear not as scenes but in the form of a relentless action that produces in the reader visions, or nightmares, of his own making.*
>
> *My means, I know, are modest and old-fashioned; my style I know is poor. And yet, I feel that I, too, must tell what follows in these pages.*
>
> *O my murdered brothers and sisters, you who sanctified God's name! I will mourn you until I die.*

SAUL TOUSTER
Brandeis University

THE HAGGADAH

Translation from the Hebrew by Yaron Peleg.
Translation from the Yiddish by Robert Szulkin and Marc Samuels.

Unless indicated that the translation was from Yiddish (pp. 47–53, 57, 65), the translation was from Hebrew.

The Arrangement of the Haggadah

The text that follows is presented with the facsimile of the original on the left-hand page, the right-hand page being devoted to translation and/or the editor's commentary. We have deviated from the original sequence of leaves on two accounts: (i) one of the original leaves in the "A" Haggadah was misplaced in its original printing and has been here correctly placed in proper sequence, as will be noted ahead; and (ii) two woodcuts have been rearranged so as to assure the continuity of text in this bilingual edition. The woodcut sequence itself remains as in the original.

The original "A" Haggadah appeared in the traditional order of Hebrew pages in leaves from right to left. Since the present facsimile follows the English order of pages from left to right, the original sequence of leaves is marked by a separate leaf number appearing at the lower right of each original page.

The Notes at the end of the book contain source references, biographical accounts, and incidental commentary, by the page. The Appendix places the "A" Haggadah in the context of Haggadah bibliography and gives its publishing history, describing its predecessor and successor editions.

PASSOVER SERVICE

MUNICH ENCLAVE

Munich, Germany, April 15-16, 1946

FROM THIS COVER of the Haggadah we learn three things: first, by the "A" insignia—of the U.S. Third Army, the Army of Occupation for Southern Germany—that the army printed it; second, by the legend and date, that it is to be used to celebrate the first Passover after the defeat of Nazi Germany; and third, by announcement of place, that all this was being done not in a DP camp but in the city of Munich. Looking inside at the text, one might ask: Where and how was the Hebrew or Yiddish type to be found in a *Judenfrei* Germany that had attempted to destroy all traces of Jewish life? By spring of 1946, Jewish voluntary agencies had brought a good deal of Hebrew and Yiddish type for the DPs in Germany. At the same time, the ICD—the Information Control Division of the American Military Government—had secured Hebrew and Yiddish type, along with other typefaces, and extensive printing facilities for use in a variety of publications including books and periodicals by or for DPs. This program was so extensive that it was characterized as "equivalent in output to a major American publishing house." One of the officers of the ICD recalled how the print facilities were secured and established for the Occupation:

> [We] would confiscate printing plants that had belonged
> to the Nazi party and individual Nazis and lease them to
> the new publishers, search out supplies of newsprint and
> ink, arrange for the salvage of bombed out presses, [and]
> supervise a swap of Bavarian cheese for British-zone zinc
> needed for making photographic plates . . .

Although some pages of the Sheinson Haggadah were made from type brought in by the Jewish agencies, other pages were made with a Hebrew typewriter. Once the zinc plates were made as described in the introduction, the army 'press,' at the instance of Klausner and using the ICD's new publishers, printed the Sheinson Haggadah, which thus became the "A" Haggadah.

סדר וציר י.ד. שטיינזון

Supplement to the Haggadah for Passover
At lower left of design, Sheinson's initials: yodh daleth shin
Page caption: Arranged and illustrated by Y. D. Sheinson

This Hebrew title page calls itself a *Supplement to the Haggadah for Passover.* The term 'Haggadah' alone, as it has evolved since the Middle Ages, has been used in a generic sense to include a variety of forms, many with contemporary references. Among them are found parodies, innovations, short abstracted versions, and extensive compendia of commentaries on the theme of deliverance or redemption of Israel. (For the place of this Haggadah in larger Haggadah bibliography, see the Appendix.) Why did Sheinson add the qualifier "Supplement"? This might suggest that he didn't intend to replace the traditional Haggadah so as to reassure the many disparate and often contending groups among the survivors who held a variety of views on religious observance. The modest qualifier, "Supplement," was not only a diplomatic gesture, but a desire for moderation and tolerance in the service of a unified Zionist position. In any event, even without using a traditional Haggadah, this Seder attracted hundreds of people from different groups. Certainly the celebratory nature of the Seder, not to mention ample fare in the context of deprivation, would move many to come.

The background design on this page, a verdant blossoming tree, suggests immediately that the *She'erith Hapletah* would enact the biblical forecast that "the remnant that is escaped of the house of Judah shall yet again take root downward, and bear fruit upward." Isaiah 37:31, I Kings 19:30.

The curly meandering lines will appear in the pages that follow to suggest fertile fields of crop or waters to be crossed to reach Zion. These life-affirming images of both nature's Eden and (especially) the Promised Land will establish the background for the parallel stories of the deliverance from slavery in Egypt and 'escape' from the Holocaust, the latter depicted at times with curly lines of smoke or flame.

PASSOVER SEDER
SERVICE

Deutsches Theatre Restaurant

Munich, Germany, April 15-16, 1946

_____

Conducting

Chaplain Abraham J. Klausner

The "Deutsches Theatre Restaurant" announced here identifies a restaurant that had been part of the Deutsches Theater in Munich since 1896 and still exists at Schwanthalerstrasse 13–15. In 1946 the restaurant had no name independent of the "Gaststätte Deutsches Theater München." It was commonly referred to by Allied personnel as the "theater restaurant" or "theater café." The Seders held there were described by Klausner as taking place in spacious rooms with a capacity of more than two hundred. Though representatives of army units, military government, and civilian DP aid agencies were present, most of those attending were DP Jews living in Munich outside of camps.

In September 1945, the army's estimate was 2,000 Jews in Munich; in April 1946 *Unzer Weg* estimated 6,000, and JDC estimated 7,000. This increase of free-living Jews had two causes. First, there was a regular flow of DPs leaving the camps and being placed in city quarters by UNRRA or JDC; and second, the flow was rising of *Brichah*-led Jews from the east heading toward Munich. Thus, the two Seders sustained the several hundred Klausner described. As for food for the Seders, Klausner's recollection is of a classic piece of 'organizing.' His agreement with the restaurant was for it to prepare and serve food he requisitioned from army stores; in return, it could keep the leftovers for its business. In a food-scarce world, everyone was happy.

The border designs in the right column contain traditional imagery of the slavery in Egypt, while in the left column the celebration of the Seder (wine, matzah, Paschal sheep) suggests that *that* slavery is long over. This Haggadah as a whole will then be about the other slavery, the contemporary disaster that is the threat to Jewish existence in Europe.

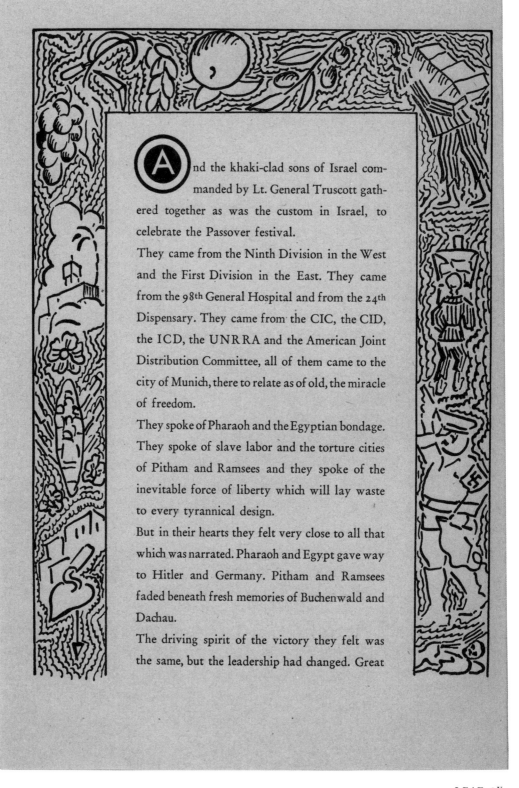

And the khaki-clad sons of Israel commanded by Lt. General Truscott gathered together as was the custom in Israel, to celebrate the Passover festival.

They came from the Ninth Division in the West and the First Division in the East. They came from the 98th General Hospital and from the 24th Dispensary. They came from the CIC, the CID, the ICD, the UNRRA and the American Joint Distribution Committee, all of them came to the city of Munich, there to relate as of old, the miracle of freedom.

They spoke of Pharaoh and the Egyptian bondage. They spoke of slave labor and the torture cities of Pitham and Ramsees and they spoke of the inevitable force of liberty which will lay waste to every tyrannical design.

But in their hearts they felt very close to all that which was narrated. Pharaoh and Egypt gave way to Hitler and Germany. Pitham and Ramsees faded beneath fresh memories of Buchenwald and Dachau.

The driving spirit of the victory they felt was the same, but the leadership had changed. Great

This Preface, written by Klausner, suggests something of his operating style. Just as he persuaded the army to permit him to organize the survivors on the ground of helping solve army security problems—a sound argument—he here colors the Seders as being for the Allied forces. A pretext certainly, for there were to be only a few representatives in khaki. Although the main body of celebrants were, we know from Klausner, to have been survivors, the Preface conveys another message, both subtle and substantive. That was the *absence* of any mention of Gen. George S. Patton who six months before had been 'fired' by Eisenhower and replaced by Gen. Lucian K. Truscott, who is mentioned in the opening sentence.

After reminding us that the survivors telling the Exodus story must have had in mind Hitler's tyrannical designs, Klausner goes on to say, with an almost harsh candor: "The driving spirit of the [Allied] victory they felt was the same, but the leadership had changed." No mention of Patton, anti-Semitic and anti-DP, who as military governor could not face the awesome new challenge, replaced by Truscott, sober and humane, who immediately expressed his awareness of the unique circumstances he faced. At his first press conference General Truscott said:

> I have left too many white crosses across North Africa, Italy, and France and I have seen too many young men wounded and maimed not to be in complete sympathy with any policy that designs to eradicate, root and branch, the evil force, Nazism, that loosed this holocaust on the world.

That he spoke of 'holocaust' long before the capitalized Holocaust was to come into use, must have been seen as a favorable harbinger—and, indeed, it was.

On this page the border design at the top begins the iteration of nature that will appear in the pages ahead—fruit, olives, grapes, flowers, crops of grain. Out of the Nazi slavery and destruction (on the right) the Jews will 'go up' to the Promised Land and do so (on the left) by sailing to palmy Jerusalem, where the trowel will build and the sickle will harvest.

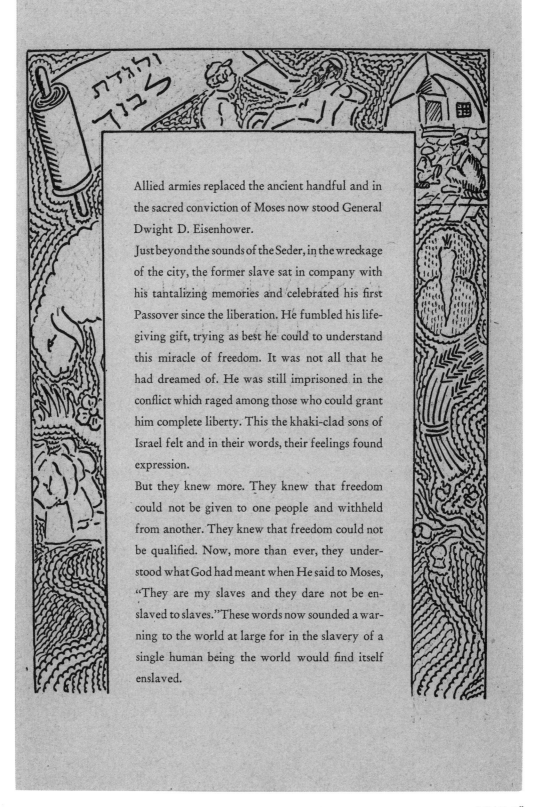

Allied armies replaced the ancient handful and in the sacred conviction of Moses now stood General Dwight D. Eisenhower.

Just beyond the sounds of the Seder, in the wreckage of the city, the former slave sat in company with his tantalizing memories and celebrated his first Passover since the liberation. He fumbled his life-giving gift, trying as best he could to understand this miracle of freedom. It was not all that he had dreamed of. He was still imprisoned in the conflict which raged among those who could grant him complete liberty. This the khaki-clad sons of Israel felt and in their words, their feelings found expression.

But they knew more. They knew that freedom could not be given to one people and withheld from another. They knew that freedom could not be qualified. Now, more than ever, they understood what God had meant when He said to Moses, "They are my slaves and they dare not be enslaved to slaves." These words now sounded a warning to the world at large for in the slavery of a single human being the world would find itself enslaved.

10

As one considers the army's Jewish chaplains who worked on behalf of the DPs during those years, one is struck by the conflicting attitudes they must have faced within the army. On one side were callous, hostile, xenophobic, if not overtly anti-Semitic, expressions; on the other, sympathetic and generous support. The large body of the officer corps probably stood somewhere between. As for feeding and medical care of DPs, there was an unambiguous willingness to aid. As for orders to requisition German housing for the DPs, the response was at times resistant if not disobedient. It is revealing to look further into the contrast between Patton and his successor Truscott—both field generals out of the old cavalry who fought together with mutual respect. What is at issue is not military skill in the field but behavior in the office of a military governor who, responsible for human survival and a civilized order, must deal with moral complexity. In his diaries, partially in response to the Harrison report on the army's failings in handling the DPs and after Eisenhower had ordered him to visit the concentration camps, Patton wrote:

> Harrison and his ilk believe that the Displaced Person is a human being, which he is not, and this applies particularly to the Jews who are lower than animals. . . . They decline, where practicable, to use latrines, preferring to relieve themselves on the floor . . .

By contrast Truscott in his memoirs notes how, on taking command, he visited and inspected the DP camps "in every part of Bavaria" and then he goes on to make observations—practical, political, humane—on various DP groups, including the Jews, reflecting on the painful complexity of the situation. No wonder the DPs and Klausner felt the sea change when they met on that Passover night to tell the Exodus story as enjoined by the Hebrew in this border design: *tell [the story] to your son.* The images are of an ancient father telling it to his son and a modern father doing the same, surrounded by Seder symbols against a background of fields of grain and harvests.

"We were slaves to Hitler in Germany . . ."

In the border design, the swastika and *Brause Bad* [the gas 'shower bath' of the crematoria] appear at the head of Nazism's works of the Holocaust, encompassing both personal modes of murder (by ax and dagger) and impersonal (by gas chamber and crematorium), all of which hover over the images of the slavery and agony of the victims. The relationship between personal killings and the impersonal killing-work of the system gets more complex when we deal with the *Einsatzgruppen*, the mobile killing squads the Nazis used in Eastern Europe as an integral part of the war-genocide machine as they swept through Russian territories. Whether personal or impersonal, the system was here able to muster men (German and other nationalities) to commit innumerable face-to-face murders.

This page design sets up referential images that parallel the Jews' oppression in the Egypt of Exodus with their slavery and death under the Nazis. The death images here are set against the life-enhancing images from the preceding and following pages: fruit, grapes, olives, grain, vegetation, flowers, the tree of life. The interplay of these images—of life and death—will pervade the border designs throughout the Haggadah, repeating themselves in various combinations, often with the addition of marginal Hebrew script that intensifies the text, such as on the preceding page—*tell [the story] to your son*. New images will be added: jars of wine, doves of peace or love, the shepherd and his flock, the Paschal lamb. A trowel will reappear as if slavery's 'making' of bricks will be turned into a creative 'laying' of bricks as home and homeland are built. A sickle will reappear amidst grain and grass to signify that the blade that cuts down in death will bring life through agriculture, clearing the ground and harvesting crops in the Promised Land.

חֲזֶרֶת

בֵּיצָה זְרוֹעַ

מָרוֹר

כַּרְפַּס חֲרוֹסֶת

קַדֵּשׁ . וּרְחַץ . כַּרְפַּס . יַחַץ .
מַגִּיד . רָחְצָה . מוֹצִיא
מַצָּה . מָרוֹר . כּוֹרֵךְ .
שֻׁלְחָן - עוֹרֵךְ צָפוּן
בָּרֵךְ . הַלֵּל . נִרְצָה .

<pre>
                    MATZAH
EGG   SHANK BONE
Betzah   Ziroa
              BITTER HERBS
                  Maror
GREENS   HAROSET
Karpas
              LETTUCE
              Hazeret
</pre>

[Order of the Seder]

Sanctify. Lave [the hands]. Greens. Divide.

Recite. Lave again. Bless over the Bread/and Matzah.
   Bitter Herbs. Combine [Matzah and Bitter Herbs].

The Meal. The Hidden [piece of Matzah].

Bless. Praise. *Nirtzah* [Prayer that Seder be properly
   observed and acceptable to God].

After the murderous images of the preceding *Brause Bad* page, the background here restores the images of fertility in the verdure of leaf, crop, flower, and grape, with the corresponding Passover symbols of the Seder's ritual. Through fertility the 'remnant' will become a whole restored people observing God's thematic command of *Genesis*: Multiply! This also echoes the Exodus story that is told in the traditional Haggadah, of how Israel in Egypt "few in number . . . became there a nation, great, mighty, and populous." Cf. Exodus 1:7; Deuteronomy 10:22, 26:5.

מַה נִּשְׁתַּנָּה הַלַּיְלָה הַזֶּה מִכָּל הַלֵּילוֹת

שֶׁבְּכָל הַלֵּילוֹת אָנוּ אוֹכְלִין חָמֵץ וּמַצָּה הַלַּיְלָה הַזֶּה כֻּלּוֹ מַצָּה

שֶׁבְּכָל הַלֵּילוֹת אָנוּ אוֹכְלִין שְׁאָר יְרָקוֹת הַלַּיְלָה הַזֶּה כֻּלּוֹ מָרוֹר.

Why is this night different from all other nights?
On all other nights we eat either leavened or unleavened bread;
why on this night only unleavened bread?
On all other nights we eat all kinds of herbs;
why on this night only bitter herbs?

The design of question marks within the borders of this and the next page announce the four traditional Passover questions.

Within the letter *Mem* that begins posing the questions (*Ma nishtana*) we see Seder symbols: a raw vegetable, a pitcher of wine, an Israelite in the desert in Exodus, a double serving dish—the 'two dishes' (*shene tashvilin*) of the customary roasted shank bone and hard-boiled egg—and matzah.

An incident during the conduct of one of these Munich Seders for DPs was especially poignant. It is told by a survivor who was there. When it came time for the young to ask the Questions, the survivor celebrants, becoming aware that there were no children present, fell silent, weeping, until one man began the asking and all the rest joined in.

שֶׁ בְּכָל הַלֵּילוֹת
אֵין אָנוּ מַטְבִּילִין
אֲפִילוּ פַּעַם אֶחָת,
הַלַּיְלָה הַזֶּה שְׁתֵּי
פְעָמִים.
שֶׁבְּכָל הַלֵּילוֹת אָנוּ
אוֹכְלִין בֵּין יוֹשְׁבִין
וּבֵין מְסֻבִּין , הַלַּיְלָה
הַזֶּה כֻּלָּנוּ מְסֻבִּין .

עֲ
בָדִים הָיִינוּ

On all other nights we need not dip our herbs even once;
why on this night do we dip twice?
On all other nights we eat either sitting up or reclining;
why on this night do we all recline?

We were slaves . . .

To the stylized Hebrew script in the margin, the *Ma nishtana* that poses the questions, is added a bristling array of question marks on this as on the preceding page—as if to ask the underlying questions of the Holocaust, the whys and hows that are in every survivor's mind. They resonated in Primo Levi's mind. *Survival in Auschwitz*, the original Italian title of which is *Se questo è un uomo* (If This Is a Man) is itself a kind of interrogatory. In chapter two he describes an incident upon his arrival at Auschwitz:

> Driven by thirst, I eyed a fine icicle outside the window, within hand's reach. I opened the window and broke off the icicle but at once a large, heavy guard prowling outside brutally snatched it away from me. '*Warum?*' I asked him in my poor German. '*Hier ist kein warum*' (there is no why here), he replied, pushing me inside with a shove.

The incident, he will tell us, haunted him thereafter.

The question mark as punctuation, which obviously did not exist in ancient Hebrew, was absorbed into Hebrew typography at least as early as the eighteenth century and is put to disturbing use here.

בן – בנימין

עֲבָדִים הָיִינוּ לְפַרְעֹה בְּמִצְרָיִם

We were slaves to Pharaoh in Egypt.

[The caption is the opening line of the Reply to the Four Questions in the traditional Haggadah. The title given by Adler was "We dug trenches in an unending circle."]

Paul Celan—born in 1920 to German-speaking Jews in Czernowitz, Romania, formerly part of Austria-Hungary—became one of the great German-language poets of the century. Having lost his family in the Holocaust and having been himself a slave laborer, he survived to reflect an embittered ambivalence about his 'mother' tongue. In this poem, he enters the inner life of slave laborers as they are depicted in this woodcut.

THERE WAS EARTH INSIDE THEM, and
they dug.

They dug and they dug, and so
their day went past, their night. And they did not praise God,
who, so they heard, wanted all this,
who, so they heard, witnessed all this.

They dug and heard nothing more;
they did not grow wise, invented no song,
invented for themselves no sort of language.
They dug.
There came then a stillness, there came also storm,
all the oceans came.
I dig, you dig, and the worm also digs,
and the singing there says: They dig.

O one, o none, o no one, o you.
Where did it go, when it went nowhere at all?
O you dig and I dig, and I dig through to you,
and the ring on our finger awakens.

בְּכָל דּוֹר וָדוֹר חַיָּב אָדָם לִרְאוֹת אֶת עַצְמוֹ כְּאִלּוּ הוּא יָצָא מִמִּצְרָיִם.

In every generation one should regard
oneself as though he had come out of Egypt.

The dramatic letter *Beth*, that begins the *Bechol dor*—'In every generation'—words that echo through the traditional Haggadah, is the *Beth* that is the first letter of the first word in the Torah, *B'rashis*. The very genesis of Genesis—'In the beginning'—this letter has occupied rabbis through generations of biblical commentary. Here the graphic *Beth* seems to encompass all the generations that came between the Exodus of Egyptian pyramids and palm trees and the Holocaust of camps, furnaces, and chimneys; and between them is the *Brause Bad*. The *Beth* may also suggest, however unwittingly, the *Brichah* in which thousands of Jews fled from the genocidal grounds of Eastern Europe to the west and on to Palestine led by the underground *Mossad Le'Aliyah Beth*. In its name—The Institute for 'B' Immigration—the letter *Beth* meant the second kind, the illegal, immigration. It was on such a *Brichah*, fleeing west, that Sheinson came to Munich. The graphic death-enclosing *Beth* stands within border designs of the Promised Land's verdure and flowing streams.

מָרוֹר זֶה שֶׁאָנוּ אוֹכְלִים עַל שׁוּם מָה. עַל שׁוּם שָׁאנוּ הלומי

קטרת הגלות, על שום שברחנו

מגלות לגלות, על שום שאמרנו:

כל אשר הגיע לאחינו תמול וכל

אשר הגיע להם בארץ מגורם לא

יגיע אלינו.

על שום שהמעטנו לעשות

לנפשנו כדי להקים את ביתנו

ומדינתנו שנחרבו.

Why do we eat this bitter herb?

Because we were intoxicated by the incense of *Galut* [Diaspora],

because we fled from one *Galut* [exile] to another,

because we reassured ourselves saying: Ours will not be the fate that befell our people before us.

Because we did little to help ourselves and reestablish our destroyed homes and country.

בן ‑ בנימין

וַיְעַנּוּנוּ וַיִּתְּנוּ עָלֵינוּ עֲבוֹדָה קָשָׁה

And they afflicted us and laid upon us hard bondage.

[The caption is from the traditional Haggadah; the title given by Adler was "We were clearing rubble."]

The captioned quotation is from chapter 1 of Exodus where the enslaved children of Israel "built for Pharaoh store-cities, Pithom and Raamses," giving Pharaoh greater power with which to oppress them. In analogous fashion, much of the Nazi construction of the concentration camps, death camps, and crematoria was done by the slave laborers themselves, thus adding to the physical torment a sickening sense that the victim's own hands were aiding the evil work. As we look at the work of the victims in this woodcut, we might ask: What could a man say to himself, or others, after such violation? Jankiel Wiernik, a carpenter at work in the camps and an underground leader, speaking to the world in an almost Dostoyevskian voice, gives a detailed account of the mass murder at Treblinka that opens with

Dear Reader...

It is for your sake that I continue to hang on to my miserable existence, though it has lost all attraction to me. How can I breathe freely and enjoy all that which nature has created?...

I sacrificed all those nearest and dearest to me. I myself took them to the execution site. I built their death chambers...

Do I look like a human being? No, definitely not. Disheveled, untidy, destroyed. It seems as if I were carrying the load of a hundred centuries on my shoulders. The load is wearisome, very wearisome, but for the time being I must bear it...

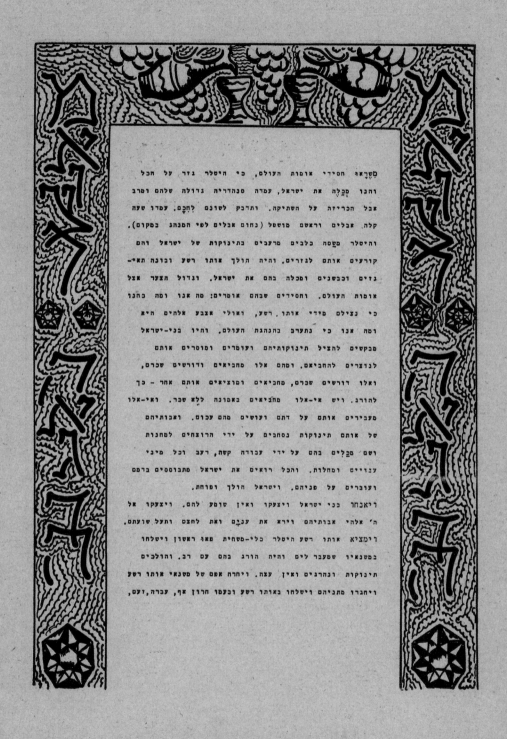

מִשָּׂרָאוּ חסידי אומות העולם, כי היטלר גזר על הכל
וחנו מכלֶּה את ישראל, עמדה סנהדריה גדולה שלהם ומרב
אבל הכריזה על השתיקה. ותדבק לשונם לְחכָּם. עמרו שעה
קלה אבלים וראשם מושפל (נחום אבלים לפי המנהג במקום).
והיטלר משֶה כלבים מרעבים בתינוקות של ישראל והם
קורעים אותם לנזרים. והיה הולך אותו רשע ובונה תאי-
גזים וכבשנים ומכלה בהם את ישראל. ונדול הצער אצל
אומות העולם. וחסידים שבהם אומרים: מה אנו ומה כחנו
כי נצילם מידי אותו. רשע, ואולי אצבע אלהים היא
ומה אנו כי נתערב בהנהגת העולם. והיו בני-ישראל
מבקשים להצל תינוקותיהם ועופרים ומוסרים אותם
לנזרים להחביאם. ומהם אלו מחביאים ודורשים שכרם,
ואלו דורשים שכר, מחביאים וסוגיאים אותם אחר - כך
להורג. ויש אי-אלו מחביאים באמונה ללא שכר. ואי-אלו
מעבירים אותם על דתם ועושים מהם עכום. ואבותיהם
של אותם תינוקות נסחבים על ידי הרוצחים למחנות
ושם מכלים בהם על ידי עבודה קשה, רעב וכל מיני
עבויים ומחלות. והכל רואים את ישראל מתבוססים ברמם
ועוברים על פניהם. וישראל הולך ופוחת.
ריאבחר בני ישראל ויצעקו ואין סומע להם. ויצעקו אל
ה' אלהי אבותיהם וירא את ענים ואת לחצם ותעל שועתם.
וימציא אותו רשע היטלר כלי-מסחית מאז ראשון וישלחו
במסנאיו שמעבר לים והיה הורג בהם עם רב. והולכים
תינוקות ונהרגים ואין עצה. ויחרח אפם של מסנאי אותו רשע
ויחגרו מתניהם וישלחו באותו רשע ובעפו חרון אף, עברה, זעם,

When the righteous among the nations of the world saw that Hitler had decided to exterminate Israel, their great assembly came together and out of their great sorrow decided to keep silent. Their tongues clove to the roofs of their mouths. And so they stood for a time like mourners with their heads bowed down (as is their custom when consoling mourners). All the while Hitler sets his hungry dogs at the babes of Israel, and they tear them to pieces. That evil man was also building gas chambers and crematoria in which to exterminate Israel. How great is the sorrow of the nations of the world! And the righteous among them say: How can we in our weakness save [Israel] from the hands of that evil man. Perhaps this is the hand of God, and who are we to interfere in the conduct of the world. And the people of Israel, in the attempt to save their children, hand them over to Christians to hide them. Some hide them for money; some, demanding money, hide them and later bring them out to be killed. And some hide them not for money, but out of conviction. And still others convert [the children] and turn them into idol worshippers. The fathers of these children are dragged by the murderers into camps, where they are made to perish by hard labor, by hunger, and by all kinds of torture and disease. And the people see how Israel is swimming in their blood but they pass by. And the number of Israel diminishes slowly. The children of Israel groaned and cried out but they were not heard. And they cried to the Lord, the God of their fathers, who saw their suffering and oppression, and their cry went up. And that man of evil, Hitler, made instruments of destruction which he sent across the sea, killing many. Babies were being killed and still no one knew what to do about it. Finally, the enemies of that man of evil grew indignant, and they girded themselves and unleashed against that man of evil and his people great wrath, rage, fury,

In the text at the end of this page and the beginning of the next Sheinson uses the language of the Haggadah that heralds God's retribution upon Egypt, echoing Psalms 78:49. But here in the twentieth century the retribution is not by God but by Allied forces.

צרת וסטלחת מלאכים רעים ויכו אותם מאתים וחמשים
טכות. וה' הקטה את לב היטלר. וכלי-מטחית מעין נטרי
ברזל ונחוטה מפטירים עלי ערי מטכנותיו אט וגפרית
והורגים בהם מאדם ועד בהמה. ורכב רב כחול הים
מכטה את ארצו טל אותו רטע ועוטה בה כלח, וישארית
הפליטה" טבמחנות-ההטגר עומדת ר"נגאלת".

שילד שלום לעולם

הרי בני ישראל הולכים ומתקבצים. ואנטי טארית הפליטה
מתכנטים מן המערות, היערות ומחנות הטמד. והם הולכים
וטבים לארץ גלותם. עם הארץ מקדם את פניהם ואומר:
טח גדול טחכם (כי כ-ט"ן רבוא טרדו ה' רבוא) ואנו
אמרנו, כי טוב אינכם בחיים, והם טולחים לאנטי טארית
הפליטה כל מיני אגרות, טיעזבו את המדינה ואף הורגים
בהם. וכני ישראל נמלטים על נפטם, מבריחים גבולות
וטם מלטטטים אותם ונוטלים את כל אטר להם, אבל
טארית הפליטה מפקירה את ממ？נה ומצילה את נפטה,
ויוצאת לגבוריה המדינה. כדי לעלות לארצנו הקדוטה.

disaster, and a band of avenging angels, afflicting them with two hundred and fifty plagues. And God hardened Hitler's heart. And instruments of destruction, eagles of iron and copper shower fire and brimstone upon his garrison cities, killing man and beast alike. And a multitude of chariots, as plenty as the sands of the sea, sweep across the land of that evil man, and destroy him, and the Holocaust survivors (*She'erith Hapletah,* the Saved Remnant) in the camps are rescued and redeemed.

WHEN PEACE CAME DOWN to earth, the people of Israel were gathering. The surviving remnants were coming out of caves, out of forests, and out of death camps, returning to the lands of their exile. The people of those lands greeted them and said: We thought you were no longer alive, and here you are, so many of you (fifty thousand out of three million). And they sent the survivors all sorts of messages, telling them to leave the land, even killing them. And the people of Israel ran for their lives; they were sneaking across borders only to be robbed of everything they had. And they abandoned their monies, and they saved their lives, and they went to Bavaria in order to go up to our Holy Land.

The number of "two hundred and fifty plagues" which are here wrought upon Hitler is based on the traditional Haggadah's ancient rabbinic extrapolation from the original ten biblical plagues. And, again, here they come not from God's divine wrath but from the material force of Allied power. The scene described concerns Polish Jewish survivors who, returning to their home, were received with a deadly anti-Semitism and then in desperation went back to Bavaria, the American zone. The number three million refers to the prewar Jewish population of Poland.

In the border designs on this page, the preceding page, and the next three pages, the Hebrew script, meaning the learning that is "the treasure [lore] of the Agada," is set against a ground of earth's treasures: gems, grapes, pitchers pouring wine, and goblets for the celebrants.

"מ שנגאלה" שארית הפליטה

עמדו לקבץ תינוקות של ישראל שנתיתמו. וכל שבט
ושבט חוסף לנפשו ועינו צרה באחרים, כי אמרו
האנשים נעשה נפשות לשבטנו. ותינוקות של ישראל
הולכים ונאספים כביצים עזובות, וגדולה המחלוקת וכל
שבט מושך לסחנהו. והתינוקות אינם עומדים בכל מיני
הפתויים, ההבטחות והנסיונות ונגררים אחד לכאן ואחד
לכאן. ויוצא שאלו שאינם חרדים חוספים תינוקות של
חרדים וחרדים חוספים תינוקות של אלו שאינם חרדים.
וכל שבט ושבט יש לו אסכולה משלו והתינוקות לומ-
דים שמה תורה. ומשלמדו זמן מה הרי הם הולכים
ומחכימים ותינוק בן יומו הרי הוא כבן שבעים והנו
מגלה דעתו בהנהגת העולם, מצות ישוב-הארץ ודברי
המדינה. ועומדים התינוקות ומתנצחים וכל אחד מתקנא
לתורתו ואח מאח נפרד, כי אינם באים לידי הסכם
בשאלת המדינה ואינם יכולים לשבת בכפיפה אחת.
ובני ארצנו הקדושה שופכים דמם בכדי להעלות ארצה
את שארית הפליטה, כי סגורים שערי הארץ: אין יוצא
ואין בא. ושליחים יוצאים מהארץ אל שארית הפליטה
ובידם כל מיני מפתחות כדי לעשות חלוקה בשארית
הפליטה ולפתח את סגר לבה. באים השליחים אל שארית
הפליטה ומסחם פוגעים בישראל הרי הם שואלים: בן
איזה שבט אתה, ואנשי שארית הפליטה תמהים ואינם
יורדים לסוף דעתם. ואף אנשי "החטיבה" שבארץ רומא
עונים: מה משמע, ישראל אנו. אומרים השליחים: ישראל

Now THAT the Saved Remnant is redeemed, the orphaned children of Israel are taken in. Each group of the Remnant makes a claim on the children and is envious of other groups on their account, because each group wants to increase its number. And while the children of Israel are being collected like abandoned eggs, the contention increases as each group tries to pull them its way. The children cannot withstand the many enticements, promises, and trials, such that some children go this way and some another. And it so happens that the non-Orthodox snatch the children of the Orthodox, and the Orthodox snatch the children of the non-Orthodox. And each and every group has its own school where children learn Torah. And after they study for a time, they grow clever; and a child behaves like a man of seventy who has opinions about how the world should be run, or how or when to settle the [Promised] Land and manage affairs of state. The children argue, and all are eager to advance their own positions and views, so that brothers are set apart, unable to agree on the question of the State [of Israel], unable to sit peacefully together.

Meanwhile the sons from our Holy Land [Palestine] shed their blood in an effort to bring survivors to Israel: for the gates of the Land are shut. No one can go in or out. And so emissaries go out from the Land [Palestine] to the surviving remnants with all kinds of keys to classify them and unlock their hearts. The emissaries come to meet the remnants, and when they meet Israel, they ask: Which group do you belong to? But the survivors do not understand them and wonder at the question. And even members of the [Jewish] Brigade in Italy reply: What is the meaning of this? Are we not, all of us, Israel? The emissaries say:

סמל היה בסח יסנתם סבעים סנה. אי אפסי בכך –
איש לסבוסו.

אומרים אנסי סארית הפליסה: וכי לא ישראל נסחם
וכי לא ישראל הוא הבונה את הארץ.
אומרים הסליחים: ישראל רק מסל היה. ארץ ישראל –
המפלגות בונות אותה.
אומרים אנסי סארית הפליסה: אנו חסיבה ה.חת, ישראל
אנו ואין אנו רוצים במפלגות.
אומרים הסליחים: אי אפסי בכך מציאות הארץ מחיבת
בכך. ובן-סלגא היה אומר: סלוג זה כסלג הוא. מה
סלני– הסים יורדים ומפלגים את הקרקע ועוסים אותה
סחוחה למען תתן כוחה, אף הפלוג מסלג את ישראל
ומסרה את הברכה. סהוא סכסיר את הקרקע לכל סיני
תורות וכל אחר הולך ונהרג על קובו סל ידר סבתותור.
הקנאות סביאה לירי גבורה וכחו סל ישראל הולך ונגרל.

ארבעה עסר לחרס ניסן סנת התס"ו בבווריה הסריכה

בכר

עברו י"ב ירחי "חירות" וסארית הפליסו
עורנה יוסבת בבווריה המדינה והיא מוסבה לסולחנה סל
אונררא. ורדס בן-פליסא : הא לחמא עניא די אכלו
אבהתנא באראע רבווריה. כל ריכפין ייתי ויכל. כל
רצריך ייתי ויפסח, ואפילו אלו סלא פסחו על אף אחד
ספתחי –ישראל בסעה סבאו עליהם להרגם. ומסלחת יוצאת

You must have been sleeping for seventy years, because the unity of Israel is a fable. It's no longer possible; each person must join a group.

The remnants answer: But was not all of Israel slaughtered together? Is not all of Israel to rebuild the land together?

The emissaries say: The unity of Israel is a fable. The land of Israel is being built by different factions.

The remnants answer: We all belong to one group, we are Israel, all of us, and we have no interest in factions.

The emissaries say: That is impossible, the reality of Israel requires it. One could argue: This rivalry is like a rivulet; just as the rivulet flows down, riving the ground and irrigating it to make it fertile, so does division divide Israel and bestow blessings on it. For it prepares the ground for all kinds of beliefs, so that people can go and die for the tip of every letter in their own torah. Thus rivalry breeds strength which increases the might of Israel.

* * * * *

Bavaria, the fourteenth day in the month of Nisan, 5706.

Twelve months of freedom have passed and the Saved Remnant is still in Bavaria, eating at the table of UNRRA. Said one of the survivors: This is the poor-man's bread our fathers ate in the land of Bavaria. Whoever need to, let them come and celebrate Passover with us, even those who did not pass over any of the houses of Israel when they were about to be killed. And a Commission goes out

The Nisan date, designating the 1946 Passover, glows with the hope of the *She'erith Hapletah*. As rabbinic commentary put it, "Nisan is the month of redemption; in Nisan Israel was redeemed from Egypt; in Nisan Israel will again be redeemed."

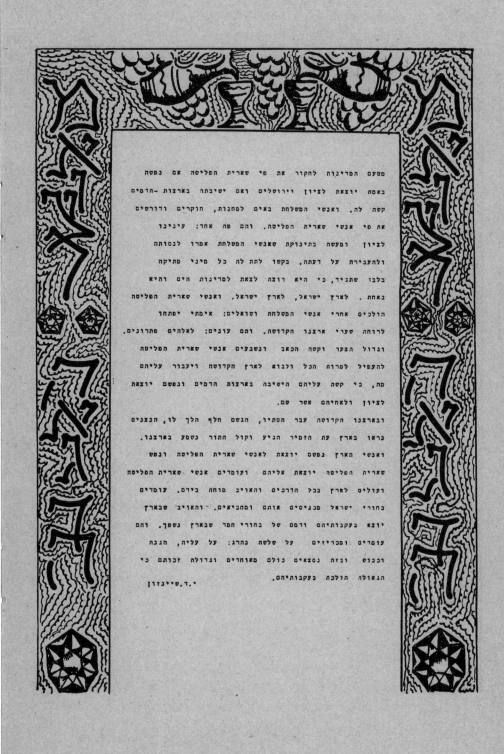

מטעם הסדינות לחקור את פי שארית הפליטה אם נפשה
באמת יוצאת לציון וירושלים ואם ישיבתה בארצות –הדפים
קשה לה. ואנשי המשלחת באים למחנות, חוקרים ודורשים
את פי אנשי שארית הפליטה. והם פה אחד: עיניכו
לציון ונפשה בתינוקת שאנשי המשלחת אמרו לנסותה
ולהעבירה על דעתה. בקשו לתת לה כל מיני פתיקה
בלבו שתגיר, כי היא רוצה לצאת לסדינות הים והיא
באחת . לארץ ישראל, לארץ ישראל. ואנשי שארית הפליטה
הולכים אחרי אנשי המשלחת ושואלים: אימתי יפתחו
לרוחה שערי ארצנו הקדושה. והם עונים: לאלהים פתרונים.
וגדול הצער וקשה הכאב ונשבעים אנשי שארית הפליטה
להעפיל לסרות הכל ולנוא לארץ הקדושה ויעבור עליהם
סה, כי קשה עליהם הישיבה בארצות הדמים ונפשם יוצאת
לציון ולאחיהם אשר שם.

ובארצנו הקדושה עבר הסתיו, הגשם חלף הלך לו, הנצנים
נראו בארץ עת הזמיר הגיע וקול התדר נשמע בארצנו.
ואנשי הארץ נפשם יוצאת לאנשי שארית הפליטה ונפש
שארית הפליטה יוצאת אליהם ועומרים אנשי שארית הפליטה
ועוליס לארץ בכל הדרכים והאויב פוחח בירם. עומדים
בחורי ישראל מכניסים אותם ומחביאים. והאויב שבארץ
יוצא בעקבותיהם ורפם של בחורי חמד שבארץ נשפך. והם
עומדים ומכריזים על שלשה נהרג: על עליה, הגנה
וכבוש ונזה נסצאים כולם מאוחדים וגדולה זכותם כי
הגאולה הולכת בעקבותיהם.   י.ד.שיינזון

on behalf of the Allies to ask the survivors whether they long for Zion and Jerusalem, and whether it is hard for them to remain in the lands that are soaked with their blood. The Commission comes to the camps, asking and inquiring of the survivors, who reply unanimously: Our eyes are set upon Zion. And it happened that the Commission tried to tempt a young girl to reply otherwise. They try to give her all sorts of sweets in the hope that she will say she wants to go to other countries. But all she says is: *Eretz Yisrael, Eretz Yisrael.* And the survivors follow the delegates and ask of them: When will the gates of our Holy Land be opened? And the Commission replies: God only knows. The sorrow is great and so is the pain, such that the survivors swear to make an illegal *Aliyah* no matter what, and go to the Holy Land at any cost; for it is hard for them to remain in lands that are soaked with their blood, and they long for Zion and their brethren there.

And in our Holy Land the autumn has passed, the rains have stopped, the buds are sprouting and the voice of the nightingale and dove are heard in the land. And the people of *Eretz Yisrael* long for the Saved Remnant, and the Saved Remnant longs for them, and the survivors come to the Land by every possible route, while the enemy protests and hinders them. The young men of Israel [Palestine] bring them in and hide them while the enemy searches for them, and the blood of the fine men of *Eretz Yisrael* is shed. Still they proclaim they will give their lives for three things: for *Aliyah,* for defense *(Haganah),* and for the taking of our rightful land. These are the principles that unite them all, and by this they merit the redemption that follows in their footsteps.

Y. D. Sheinson

The Commission referred to is the Anglo-American Committee of Inquiry established in December 1945 by the British and American governments to direct attention to the future of the Jewish DPs and policy toward Palestine. The Committee's conduct in making inquiries among the DPs was pretty much as described. Its report, never implemented, was superseded by political events leading to Israel's establishment in 1948.

בן - בנימין

זָכַרְנוּ אֶת "הַדָּגָה" ...

We remember the fish. . . .

[The caption comes from the Book of Numbers 11:5,
where the Israelites in the wilderness, unsatisfied with
the *manna* divinely given them, hanker for their days of
slavery in Egypt and hunger for 'flesh.' The title
given by Adler was "Reward for our labor."]

Compared with the other woodcuts that are so full of pain and death, this scene of feeding time is more peaceful, despite the death-mask faces, as if those near death could be sustained by memories of sharing food. Even the so-called work Jews, kept alive for their labor in some of the camps, were slowly starved. Primo Levi, as a chemist, was an important worker and thus had a better, if bare subsistence, diet. But he saw the starved and starving all around him and here he bears witness in the opening passages of his poem, *Shemà*.

You who live secure
In your own houses,
Who return at evening to find
Hot food and friendly faces:

   Consider whether this is a man,
   Who labors in the mud
   Who knows no peace
   Who fights for a crust of bread
   Who dies at a yes or a no.
   Consider whether this is a woman,
   Without hair or name
   With no more strength to remember
   Eyes empty and womb cold
   As a frog in winter.

Consider this has been:

   . . .

ב

רוך שומר הבטחתו

לישראל. ברוד בלפור שחשב

לעשות את הקץ. לעשות כמו

שנאמר: ידע תדע כי שוב

לא יענו אתכם ארבע מאות

שנה ובית יקום לכם כמו

שנאמר: אל יהיה זרעך גר

בארץ לא להם.

ב

רוד שומר הבטחתו

לישראל וחבר את הספר

הלבן, אסר על העליה וקנית

הקרקעות וחשב לעשות את

הקץ.

BLESSED be He who keeps His promise to Israel. Blessed be Balfour who intended to hasten the end [of *Galut*] and to do as it is said: Know that you shall be no more oppressed for four hundred years, and a house shall be built for you, as it is said: Your seed shall not be sojourners in a land that is not theirs.

BLESSED be he who keeps his promise to Israel, who wrote the White Paper, forbade *Aliyah* and the purchase of land, and who intended to hasten the end.

The second paragraph is hard to interpret. The White Paper apparently refers to that of May 1939 by which the British effectively withdrew the 1917 Balfour Declaration. Is the "blessing" here meant satirically, pointing not to the keeping but to the breaking of a promise? In that case, if Balfour "intended to hasten the end [of Galut]," those who wrote the recent White Paper would have "intended to hasten the end" of the promise itself.

The border designs on this page and the next succeeding page render a Zion that is truly a Promised Land from which flower and leaf, pomegranate and palm, grape and grain rise above the flowing stream with loving doves, and grazing ram at peace. It is a biblical vision, as when the Israelites were suffering in the Wilderness and Moses sent scouts into the Land of Canaan, and they came back with the words: *We came unto the land whither thou sentest us, and surely it floweth with milk and honey; and this is the fruit of it.* Numbers 13:27. The single palm tree which appears here as in other border designs, and the clusters of grape, must surely carry the figure of the Song of Songs, where Solomon sings: *How fair and how pleasant art thou, O love, for delights? / This thy stature is like to a palm tree, and thy breasts to clusters of grapes . . . the pomegranates bud forth: there will I give thee my loves.* 7:6, 7, 12. Thus the body of the bride and Jerusalem are joined.

41

בן – בנימין

וַיַּעֲבִדוּ אֶת בְּנֵי יִשְׂרָאֵל בְּפָרֶךְ:

And they afflicted the children of Israel with hard bondage.

[The caption is from the traditional Haggadah. The title given by Adler was "We were hauling logs."]

One could imagine how a prisoner, surrounded by death and the detritus of camp and workshop and the befouled air he breathes in, might dream of the countryside. And so it was that Frank (Franek) Stiffel in Auschwitz found himself volunteering for Kobier, a sub-camp 50 km. distant, in a centuries-old forest of oak and needle trees. He tells us in his memoir what he thought on the first day's march out of camp. *Maybe Kobier meant just agricultural work. To work on a farm! Heavy work? So what! A farm meant plenty of fresh air and sun, and the smell of freedom, and food!* But it is still Auschwitz. Morning report. The count. The group forms up and marches out into the woods with a *dozen SS Postens walking in front, behind and at both sides of us.* There are two warnings on pain of death: *to cross the Postenkette* [the 'chain of guards' that marks the work borders], and *to touch the healthy trees.* So, on sick or broken or marked trees, he spends his morning *sawing, cutting, barking, and being beaten by a foreman.* Noon: *a bowlful of soup . . . with stone-hard kernels of old corn.* Afternoon, logs: *lifting, running, stack building, and again running and lifting. My shoulders . . . sore and my feet swollen.* The march back. Evening report. *[B]ecause we are considered a heavy work detail . . . [we get a] portion of moldy bread and liverwurst.* He will have one adventure getting to a farm and 'organizing' some sandwiches from a sympathetic farmer; he will sneak pleasurable glimpses of greenery and blue sky; and he will realize that you don't have to cross the *Kette* for a guard to shoot you and drag your body beyond the *Kette* so as to earn a bonus for having stopped an 'escapee.' Stiffel's life was much like the picture shown in this woodcut.

חכם מה הוא אומר

מה הארץ והמדינה שנטשכם יוצאת אליהם? וכי אין ביתי
ביתכם? וכי אין כל רחבי המדינה לפניכם ואני בל
אדע ארץ בה נשם אדם לרוחה כבארצי. ואף אתה אמר לו:
אתה הלא היית הראשון, שבצר לך צעקת "למטן הטולרת",
אף אנו צר לנו ויש לנו צרך במולרת. כל אומה
ושמחותה שבטחונות מותרת במולרת ולעם עתיק ומטפח שבעטים
אסור היכן מצינו? אף אתה אמר לו: מי יודע כמה
זמן יעברו לנו חסדיך וזרועתך המדינה עלינו. בית
ומדינה לא חסד הם לנו כי אם זכות.

רשע מה הוא אומר

וכי צרה לכם הארץ שאתם נרחקים לארץ ישראל. הלא כל
הארץ לפניכם, והעיקר שיש לכם שליחות נעלה. לכו
בכחכם ובנו את אירופה ההרוסה. אף אתה הקהה את שני
ואמר לו: נתנו חילנו לאירופה והנה בנו לנו תאי-
נזים ומשרפות, כלו בנו בכל מיני המצאות אכזריות וכי
בעבור זה נבנה שוב את אירופה. אף אתה אמר לו: אלו
היה שם והיה "נגאל" לא היה כופר בעיקר סאומתו
נלחמה עליו בחרוף נפש – בית ומדינה . . .

תם מה הוא אומר

מה זאת? וכי בארץ כה קטנה תכנסו? ומה יהיה על
ישמעאל? ואמרת אליו: לא בחזק יד ובנצול הזולת אנו
בונים את ביתנו. מהשממה הוצאנו לחם. ואשר לישמעאל –
ישראל לא יקפח את זכותו.

ושא ינו יודע לשאל   אתה פתח לו.

WHAT DOES THE WISE SON SAY?

What is this land and State that you long for? Is not my house your house? Is not this whole country open before you; why, I do not know another country where men can breathe more freely. You should tell him: Were you not the first to cry out 'for home and country' at the time of your need? Well, this is the hour of our need, and we demand a homeland. Every nation, even the least and lowest, is permitted to have a homeland, whereas a people as ancient and neglected as we are is not permitted. How could this be justified? You should tell him: Who knows how long their charity and their protective arm shall be extended to us? A home and a country should not come out of charity but by right.

WHAT DOES THE WICKED SON SAY?

Is there no room for you here that you should scramble into the land of Israel? Why, the whole world is open before you. And what's more, you have a mission: go and use your strength to rebuild a devastated Europe. You should set his teeth on edge and tell him: We have already given our best to Europe, and in return they built gas chambers and crematoria, and exterminated us with cruel ingenuity. Should we, for all this, rebuild Europe? You should tell him: Had they been in our place and been saved, they wouldn't have renounced the very cause for which they fought so bravely, that is, for a home and a country . . .

WHAT DOES THE SIMPLE SON SAY?

What is this? Why do you want to huddle in so small a land? And what about Ishmael? You should tell him: We are not building our houses with a mighty hand by the exploitation of others. We made bread out of the wilderness. And as for Ishmael, Israel will not overlook his rights.

AND FOR THE SON WHO IS TOO YOUNG TO KNOW HOW TO ASK,

you should begin by saying:

אס יידישע פֿאלק
פֿאלגעדענקט אין א משך פֿון
טויזענטער יארן דעם טאג ווען
עס איז ארויס פֿון דער קנעכט-
שאפֿט. דורך פֿארשקלאפֿונג
צוואנג, אינקוויזיציע, אויסראטונג
און אומרוען טראגט דאס יידי
שע פֿאלק אין האַרצן די
בײַנקשאפֿט נאך פֿרײַהייט.
און האט דאס אלויסגעזאגט
אין א פֿאלקסטימלעכן אויס
דרוק, וועלכער לאזט ניט
פֿארבײַ קיין אײן יידישע
נשמה קיין געפֿלאגט און
געפֿײניגט זײל.

[Yiddish]

For thousands of years the Jewish People have commemorated the day of their Exodus from bondage. Through slavery, force, inquisition, destruction, and troubles, the Jewish People have borne in their hearts a longing for freedom and expressed this longing universally so as not to leave out a single tormented Jewish soul.

On the preceding page, the Hebrew text advises the father on how he should speak to his four sons—the wise son, the wicked son, the simple son, and the son too young to know how to ask. To the too-young-to-ask son, the father is told to explain, as this page demonstrates, in *Yiddish*—the *Mamaloshen* (mother tongue) of household speech. Sheinson's idea is by no means original. As early as the eleventh century there was some rabbinic opinion that the answer to the Four Questions should be in the vernacular.

In the border designs, the images move from the lower right as refugees go up toward the map of Palestine, toward the mountains and palms, toward the walled city of Jerusalem, toward where deer cavort freely in the woodland and the palm fronds give shade.

פון עלטערן צו קינדער .פון
דור צו דור ווערט איבער-
געגעבן די געשיכטע פון
יציאת מצרים ווי א פער-
זענלעכע דערינערונג, ווערט
ניט פארבלאסט און
בלאקט ניט אפ.
„בכל דור ודור חיב
אדם לראות את עצמו
כאילו הוא יצא ממצרים".
סאיז ניטא קיין העכערע
היסטארישע באוווסטזיניקייט
ווי אט די . סאיז ניטא קיין
טאפאלערע צוזאמענגיסונג
פון יחיד מיטן כלל - סיי
אויפן גאנצן ערד קוגל און
אין די טיפעניטן פון דורות-

[Yiddish]

From parents to children, from generation to generation, the story of the Exodus from Egypt is passed on as a personal memory; it never pales or loses its luster.

"In each and every generation one should regard oneself as though he had come out of Egypt." There is no higher historical consciousness than this. There is no more complete fusing of the individual and the community to be found on the face of the earth and in the depths of the generations than this.

In this border design, slavery in Egypt is depicted by a taskmaster with club and whip driving the Jewish slaves in their heavy work of hauling slabs and pushing wheelbarrows full of bricks—which event, miraculously, is transformed to the Passover symbols of wine, matzah, and Paschal sheep. The club and whip signify the bondage of the Nazi terror with its pervasive beatings by guards, Kapos, and taskmasters.

וואס זאל זײַן גרעסער ווי
די וועלכע ליגט אין דעם
אלטן פעדאגאגישן
געבאט.
איז דען דא א ליטערא-
רישערע שאפונג, וועל-
כע דערבײַט צו עקל צו
דער קנעכטשאפט, צו
פרײַהייט ליבע, מער
ווי די געשיכטע פון
פארשקלאפונג און
יציאת מצרים ?
איז דען דא אן אלטע
דערינערונג, וואס זאל זײַן
דער סימבאל פאר דער
געגנוואַרט און צוקונפט

[Yiddish]

Can anything be greater than the wisdom of the ancient commandment?

Is there anything in the wisdom literature that better teaches us to hate and despise slavery and to love freedom, than the story of the bondage and exodus from Egypt?

Does there exist any ancient memory that could serve as symbol for the present and future [better than this]:

In contrast to the preceding page designs that picture the exodus from Egypt and the Seders memorializing it, the images here render the passage *today* to the Promised Land. Beginning at the lower right, Hitler stands on a corpse, presiding over the enslaved Jews who push wheelbarrows of bricks and haul slabs as they head toward (or dream of) a verdant land. On the other side, ascending, the trowel will transform the enslavement of brickworks into the creative labor of building a homeland. The wavering meander lines are once again a background of both fruitful nature and the seas that boatloads will cross to come to the Promised Land.

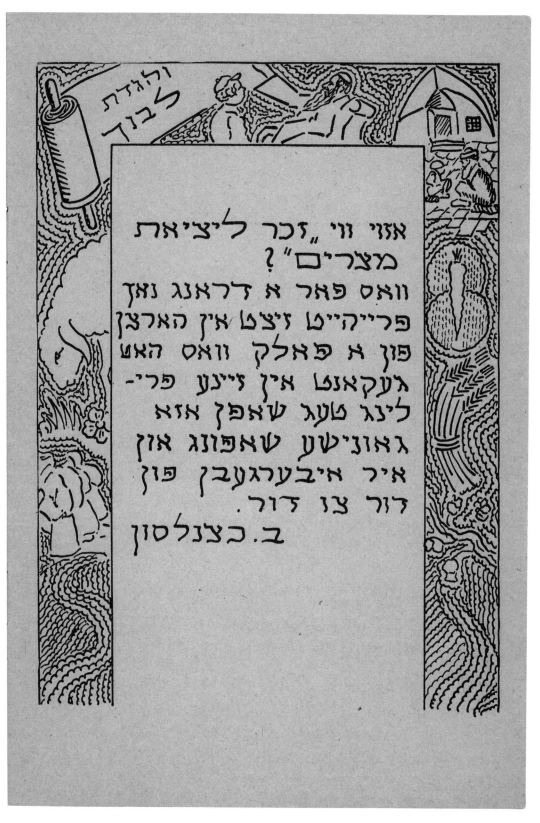

אזוי ווי „זכר ליציאת
מצרים"?
וואס פאר א דראנג נאך
פרייהייט זיצט אין הארצן
פון א פאלק וואס האט
געקאנט אין זייגע פרי־
ליגג טעג שאפן אזא
גאונישן שאפונג און
איר איבערגעבן פון
דור צו דור.
ב. כצנלסון

[Yiddish]

"Remembrance of the Exodus from Egypt."

What a thirst for freedom lies in the heart of a People who could, in its springtime, bring forth such an ingenious creation and transmit it from generation to generation.

B. Katznelson

Berl Katznelson (b. Russia 1887, d. Palestine 1944) was a central figure of the Second Aliyah, leader of the Zionist Labor movement, educator, and writer. He exercised a tremendous influence on the political ideas on which the State of Israel was eventually founded.

בן - בנימין

שֶׁלֹּא אֶחָד בִּלְבַד עָמַד עָלֵינוּ לְכַלּוֹתֵינוּ

It was not just one alone who has risen up to destroy us.

[The caption is from the traditional Haggadah; the title given by Adler was "Move! Move! They drive us because the liberators are approaching."]

The image of the forced march rendered in this woodcut as a kind of traveling charnel house has earned its name: 'death march.' Even an American soldier liberating a camp came to understand this meaning:

> [M]any of the new prisoners had recently been forced to march from the vicinity of Hungary to Gunskirchen [Lager]. There was very little food. If they fell out and were too weak to continue, the SS men shot them. The airline distance from the Hungarian border . . . is 150 miles. The intervening territory is full of mountains and winding roads, so the actual distance was far greater than 150 miles. It is not hard to imagine the thousands of skeletons that mark their route.

Miklós Radnóti, the poet, knew it from the inside. His last march was with 3,600 fellow slave laborers. Only 800 survived but for want of housing they were forced to dig a ditch, were shot, and then buried in a mass grave. Later when the bodies were exhumed, on Radnóti's body were found his last poems, among them this one, *Forced March*, opening with:

> *Crazy. He stumbles, flops, gets up   and trudges on again.*
> *He moves his ankles and his knees   like one wandering pain,*
> *then sallies forth, as if a wing   lifted where he went,*
> *and when the ditch invites him in,   he dare not give consent . . .*

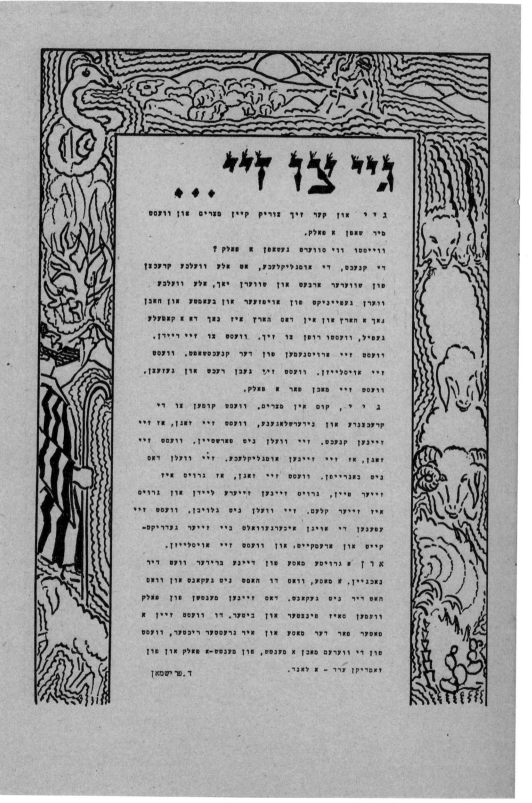

גיי צו זיי...

...

ג י י, און קער זיך צוריק קיין מצרים און וועט
מיר מאכן א פאלק.

ווייסטו ווי סווערס געשאפן א פאלק ?

די קנעכט, די אומגליקלעכע, אט אלע וועלכע קרעכצן
פון שווערער ארבעט און שווערן יאך, אלע וועלכע
ווערן געפייניקט פון אויסמיער און באמסע און האבן
נאך א הארץ און אין דאס הארץ איז נאך דא א קאפעלע
געפיל, וועסטו רופן צו זיך, וועסט צו זיי ריידן.
וועסט זיי ארויסנעמען פון דער קנעכטשאפט, וועסט
זיי אויסלייזן, וועסט זיי געבן רעכט און געזעצן.
וועסט זיי מאכן פאר א פאלק.

ג י י, קום אין מצרים, וועסט קומען צו די
קרעכצנדע און נידערגעשלאגנע, וועסט זיי זאגן, אז זיי
זיינען קנעכט, זיי וועלן ניס פארשטיין, וועסט זיי
זאגן, אז זיי זיינען אומגליקלעכע, זיי וועלן דאס
ניט באגרייפן, וועסט זיי זאגן, אז גרויס איז
זייער סיין, גרויס זיינען זייערע ליידן און גרויס
איז זייער קלעם, זיי וועלן ניס גלויבן, וועסט זיי
ספעגנען די אויגן איבערגעוואלס ביי זייער געדריקס-
קיים און ארקסקיים, און וועסט זיי אויסלייזן.
א ך א גרויסע מאסע פון דיינע ברידער וועס דיר
נאכגיין, א מאסע, וואס דו האסט ניס געקאנס און וואס
האס דיר ניס געקאנס. דאס זיינען מענסשן פון פאלק
וועמפען סאיז מינצטער און ביטער. דו וועסט זיין א
מאסער סאר דער מאסע און איר גרעסטער ריכטער, וועסט
פון די ווערעם מאכן א מענסס, פון מענטסט-א פאלק און פון
זאמדיקן ערד - א לאנד.

ד. פרישמאן

[Yiddish]

GO TO THEM . . .

Go back to Egypt and I shall make a nation out of you.

Do you know how a Nation is created?

The slaves, groaning in their misery, all those who moan from heavy labor and heavy yoke, all those who are tortured by overseers and taskmasters, and yet retain a heart, and in that heart a spark of feeling, all of them you shall summon to come. You shall speak to them. You shall lead them out of bondage. You shall redeem them. You shall give them rights and laws. You shall make of them a Nation.

Go, come to Egypt. You shall come to those groaning and downtrodden. You shall say to them that they are slaves. They will not understand. You shall tell them that they are the unfortunates ones. They will not understand. You shall say to them that great is their pain, great are their sufferings, and great is their plight. They will not believe. You shall with force open their eyes to their oppression and suffering, and you shall redeem them.

And a great crowd of your brethren will follow you. A crowd whom you did not know and who did not know you. These are the people who live in misery and pain. You shall be a father to them and their greatest judge; you shall form men and women out of these worms, and a Nation out of them, and out of the sandy soil you shall make a land.

D. Frischmann

David Frischmann (1859–1922), a Pole, was a leading figure in modern Hebrew, writing poetry, short stories, essays, and criticism, and editing several journals.

This page's border designs depict scenes from the life of Moses: as shepherd keeping his flock; standing with staff in hand, facing the burning bush; and, above it, the serpent wrapping around the staff. The last image is from Numbers 21:6–9 where the serpent and staff stand for both the chastisement of Israel and a sign of healing when looked upon, presumably, with faith. This is the same sign—the snake entwining the rod—as that evolved among the Greeks to become, in the caduceus, the emblem of the physician's vocation of healing.

It is this promise that has helped our fathers and us. It is not just one alone who has risen up to destroy us; for they have risen up to destroy us in each and every generation. Still the Holy One, blessed be He, saves us from their hand.

The Hebrew script in the border design declares "This is our faith"—*Vehi emunateynu*. Coming as it does from the fragment of a page, or shard of a scroll, the voice must be that of the Saved Remnant, the *She'erith Hapletah*. "This is our faith."

Where in other places Sheinson's bitterness as a survivor seemed to turn him away from God, here he takes the above text from the Haggadah liturgy as the strongest declaration of faith the survivor can make.

בן - בנימין

שְׁפַּרְעֹה לֹא גָזַר אֶלָּא עַל הַזְּכָרִים
וְלָבָן בִּקֵּשׁ לַעֲקֹר אֶת הַכֹּל:

While Pharaoh decreed death only for the male children,
Laban sought to uproot all.

[The caption is from the traditional Haggadah, referring to
Pharaoh (Exodus 1:16,22) and to Laban (Genesis 31:29).
The title given by Adler was "Selection."]

'Selections' during the Holocaust meant death and occurred everywhere at any time. Some might have been as imaged here in this
woodcut: the SS man in black at the railway's end, selecting for life
or death the cargo of Jews disgorged from the boxcars. Or, it might
have been on the streets of Warsaw at noon in a roundup. Or, in a
night sweep of homes in Lvov. Or, in the making of a list by a *Juden-
rat* or Kapo to fill a quota. Or, in the decision of who will have how
much bread? Perhaps the earliest culture-forming 'selection' was
Pharaoh's selection of newborn Jewish males for death, as is suggested by this caption. For Primo Levi, 'selection' placed him
among the healthy who were sent off to work, while they looked
back and *our women, our parents, our children disappeared . . . as an
obscure mass at the other end of the platform; then we saw nothing more.*
How then could the survivors think they were Chosen? To all these
'selections,' we might find the universal epitaph composed by the
poet-survivor, Dan Pagis.

> *Written in Pencil in a Sealed Railway-Car*
>
> *here in this transport*
> *I Eve*
> *with Abel my son*
> *if you see my older son*
> *Cain son of Adam*
> *tell him that I*

The poem ends without punctuation.

דַיֵּנוּ.

אָלּוּ פְזְּרָנוּ בֵּין הַגּוֹיִים וְלֹא נָתַן לָנוּ גְזֵירוֹת מִסְעַ-
צְלָב רִאשׁוֹן דַיֵּנוּ. אִלּוּ נָתַן לָנוּ גְזֵירוֹת מִסְעַ-צְלָב רִאשׁוֹן
וְלֹא נָתַן לָנוּ גְזֵירוֹת מִסְעַ-צְלָב שֵׁנִי דַיֵּנוּ. אִלּוּ נָתַן
לָנוּ גְזֵירוֹת מִסְעַ-צְלָב שֵׁנִי וְלֹא נָתַן לָנוּ עֲלִילַת דָם
דַיֵּנוּ. אָלּוּ נָתַן לָנוּ עֲלִילַת דָם וְלֹא נָתַן לָנוּ רְדִיפוֹת
מִסְעַ-צְלָב שְׁלִישִׁי דַיֵּנוּ. אִלּוּ נָתַן לָנוּ רְדִיפוֹת מִסְעַ-צְלָב
שְׁלִישִׁי וְלֹא נָתַן לָנוּ "אוֹת קָלוֹן" דַיֵּנוּ. אָלּוּ נָתַן לָנוּ
"אוֹת-קָלוֹן" וְלֹא נָתַן לָנוּ גְזֵירַת "הַמַּגֵּפָה הַשְּׁחוֹרָה" דַיֵּנוּ.
אָלּוּ נָתַן לָנוּ אֶת גְזֵירַת הַמַּגֵּפָה הַשְּׁחוֹרָה וְלֹא נָתַן לָנוּ אֶת
הָאִינְקְוִיזִיצְיָה דַיֵּנוּ. אָלּוּ נָתַן לָנוּ אֶת הָאִינְקְוִיזִיצְיָה
וְלֹא נָתַן לָנוּ גְזֵירוֹת ת"ח וְת"ס דַיֵּנוּ. אָלּוּ נָתַן לָנוּ
גְזֵירוֹת ת"ח וְת"ס וְלֹא נָתַן לָנוּ אֶת שְׁחִיטוֹת תרע"ס
בְּאוּקְרַינָה דַיֵּנוּ. אָלּוּ נָתַן לָנוּ אֶת הַשְּׁחִיטוֹת בְּאוּקְרַינָה
וְלֹא נָתַן לָנוּ אֶת הִיטְלֶר דַיֵּנוּ. אָלּוּ נָתַן לָנוּ אֶת
הִיטְלֶר וְלֹא הֵקִימוּ לָנוּ נַסָּאוֹת דַיֵּנוּ. אָלּוּ הֵקִימוּ לָנוּ
נַסָּאוֹת וְלֹא הֵקִימוּ לָנוּ תָאֵי – גָזִים וְכַבְשָׁנִים דַיֵּנוּ.
אָלּוּ הֵקִימוּ לָנוּ תָאֵי – גָזִים וְכַבְשָׁנִים וְלֹא הִתְעַלְּלוּ
בְּנָשֵׁינוּ וּבְטַפֵּנוּ דַיֵּנוּ. אִלּוּ הִתְעַלְּלוּ בְּנָשֵׁינוּ וּבְטַפֵּנוּ
וְלֹא הֶעֱבִידוּנוּ בְּפֶרֶךְ דַיֵּנוּ. אִלּוּ הֶעֱבִידוּנוּ בְּפֶרֶךְ
וְלֹא כִלּוּ בָּנוּ בְּרָעָב דַיֵּנוּ. אִלּוּ כִלּוּ בָּנוּ בְּרָעָב
וְלֹא כִלּוּ בָּנוּ בְּכָל מִינֵי מַחֲלוֹת וַעֲנוּיִים דַיֵּנוּ.

עַל אַחַת כַּמָּה וְכַמָּה מַשֶׁהִגִּיעַ לָנוּ כָּל אֵלֶּה
הֲרֵי אָנוּ חַיָּבִים לַעֲלוֹת, לְהַעְפִּיל, לְחַסֵל אֶת הַגָּלוּת.
לִבְנוֹת אֶת אֶרֶץ הַבְּחִירָה וּלְהָקִים בַּיִת לָנוּ וּלְבָנֵינוּ
עַד עוֹלָם.

DAYENU

We would have been content.

Had He scattered us among the nations but had not given us the First Crusade, we would have been content. Had He given us the First Crusade but not the Second, we would have been content. Had He given us the Second Crusade but not the Blood Libel, we would have been content. Had He given us the Blood Libel but not the persecutions of the Third Crusade, we would have been content. Had He given us the persecutions of the Third Crusade, but not the Badge of Shame, we would have been content. Had He given us the Badge of Shame but not the persecutions of the Black Plague, we would have been content. Had He given us the persecutions of the Black Plague but not the Inquisition, we would have been content. Had He given us the Inquisition but not the pogroms of 1648–49, we would have been content. Had He given us the pogroms of 1648–49 but not the slaughter of 1919 in Ukraine, we would have been content. Had He given us the slaughter in Ukraine but not Hitler, we would have been content. Had He given us Hitler but no ghettos, we would have been content. Had He given us ghettos but no gas chambers and crematoria, we would have been content. Had He given us gas chambers and crematoria, but our wives and children had not been tortured, we would have been content. Had our wives and children been tortured but we had not been forced into hard bondage, we would have been content. Had we been forced into hard bondage but not been made to die of hunger, we would have been content. Had we been made to die of hunger but not of disease and torture, we would have been content.

All the more so, since all these have befallen us, we must make *Aliyah,* even if illegally, wipe out the *Galut,* build the chosen land, and make a home for ourselves and our children for eternity.

This *dayenu* recites not God's blessings, as is traditional, but visitations of affliction, a veritable anti-Hallel. The conclusion replaces the hope of God's deliverance with a vision of 'ourselves' working for Zion. See the Introduction, pages xxviii–xxix.

In the side borders, the Hebrew script echoes *dayenu* ('We would have been content') as the uplifted hands with tallith-like sleeves at the top seem to express beseechment or resignation.

ניטא קיין
שלעכטער און גוטער
גלות. יעדער
גלות פירט צום
אונטערגאנג.

מיט בלוט
פון אונדזער הארץ
ביים ליכט פון
אונדזער גלויבן
און מיט דער
לעצטער האפנונג
וועלק מיר דורך-
ברעכן יעדע
וואנט, דורכברעכן
און עולה זיין.

[Yiddish]

There is no such thing as a 'bad' or 'good' exile. Every exile leads to extinction.

With the blood of our hearts, by the light of our faith, and with a final hope, we shall break through every wall. We shall break through and go up [to the Land of Israel].

The border designs are of ships sailing (illegally at the time) over the seas toward a Palestine that is represented by three stylized maps with an open harbor. That open harbor would, with the founding of Israel in 1948, welcome many more ships making a legal way to the Promised Land. Despite this, the DP camps would continue with 'hard case' Jews lingering in ever diminishing numbers. The 'hard cases' were those who, not wanting to go to Israel, were too sick or too old to be accepted into a country even where they were seeking to join other family members; or were waiting for acceptable guarantors, or the resolution of bureaucratic foul-ups, or other legal process; or had criminal records or diseases that barred them from immigration; or refused to break up families when one person was barred; or were disgruntled, undecided, or uncooperative. These cases were finally 'cleared' through the efforts of JDC, HIAS, ORT (Organization for Rehabilitation through Training), and OSE (*Oeuvre Secours pour Enfants*), and the last camp, Foehrenwald, was closed on February 28, 1957. Of the 300,000 Jewish DPs—50,000 originally liberated in Germany and Austria, plus 250,000 from Poland, the Soviet Union, and other European countries—Yehuda Bauer estimates "Roughly speaking, two thirds went to Israel, and the rest elsewhere."

בן - בנימין

לְפִיכָךְ אֲנַחְנוּ חַיָּבִים ...

Therefore, we are bound. . . .

[This caption, from the traditional Haggadah liturgy, continues with *to thank, praise, laud, glorify, exalt . . . Him who performed all these miracles for our fathers and us*—a painful irony here. The original title given by Adler was "Home! Home?"]

O the chimneys. The poet Nelly Sach's cry, or sigh, or lament echoes in the air like a low thunder. And the smoke, curling from the stacks toward the heavens, contains the spirits of the dead that counsel and perhaps console the living. Carved into the heavens in this woodcut are God's words to Abraham—*Lekh lekha . . . el ha'aretz* ["Go you forth . . . to the land . . ."] Genesis 12:1. But the image here is not so much emblematic of the words of divine promise as a warning from the departed souls lost to the crematoria, souls that rose up through the chimneys and are rising now to the heavens. *Aliyah!* Go up! Jacob Glatstein, the great Yiddish poet who 'survived' in North America, saw something like this when he wrote that *The cloud-Jew writes Yiddish letters/ on an alien sky.* In another poem, *Smoke,* the poet gathered smoke, clouds, and psalm:

> *Through crematorium chimneys*
> *a Jew curls toward the God of his fathers . . .*
> *Upward, toward the heavens*
> *sacred smoke weeps, yearns.*
> *God—where You are—*
> *we all disappear.*

שְׁפֹךְ
חֲמָתְךָ

עַל הַגּוֹיִם אֲשֶׁר
לֹא יְדָעוּךָ וְעַל
הַמַּמְלָכוֹת אֲשֶׁר
בְּשִׁמְךָ לֹא קָרָאוּ:
כִּי אָכַל אֶת יַעֲקֹב
וְאֶת נָוֵהוּ הֵשַׁמּוּ:
שְׁפָךְ עֲלֵיהֶם זַעְמֶךָ
וַחֲרוֹן אַפְּךָ יַשִּׂיגֵם:
תִּרְדֹּף בְּאַף
וְתַשְׁמִידֵם מִתַּחַת
שְׁמֵי יְיָ:

POUR OUT THY WRATH upon the nations that know Thee not, and upon the kingdoms that do not know Thy name. For they have devoured Jacob and laid waste his habitation. Pour out Thy indignation upon them, and let the fierceness of Thy anger overtake them. Pursue them in anger and destroy them under the heavens of the Lord.

The text from the Haggadah derives from Psalms 79:6–7 and 69:25 and Lamentations 3:66.

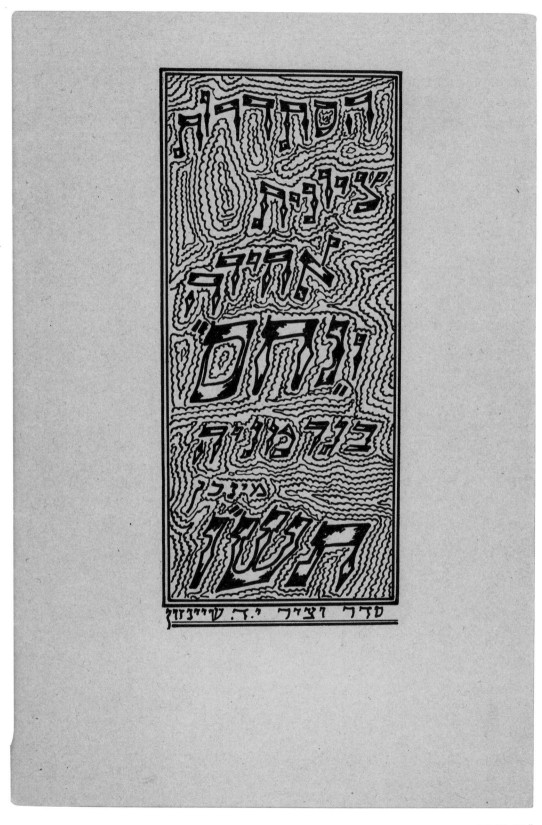

United Zionist Organization

and

"NHM"

Germany

Munich
5706
[1946]

Arranged and illustrated by Y. D. Sheinson

The acronym *NHM (Nocham)* stands for *Noar Halutzi Meuhad*
(United Pioneer Youth) and means literally "consolation."

To mr. & mrs. Tauster as a
reminder that they and
others made it possible for
our people to leave germany
and live as free men and
women in Israel.

Joe Levine

On August 4, 1945, some thirteen weeks after the liberation of the Dachau camps, the JDC established its offices in Munich and began its work in Bavaria to aid the Saved Remnant. In September other JDC workers were brought in, among them Joe Levine who was assigned to an UNRRA team in eastern Bavaria. During most of the next year he was stationed in Regensburg, often working with Klausner. For Passover 1946, he attended the first Seder with the young DPs in 'Kibbutz' *Nocham* in Regensburg. On the next night he apparently attended Klausner's Seder in Munich, one of the JDC representatives mentioned by Klausner in his Preface.

In May 1952 the editor's father, Ben Touster, was elected president of the Hebrew Immigrant Aid Society (HIAS), the organization founded at the turn of the century by American refugees and devoted over the years to the rescue and care of millions of Jews in jeopardy worldwide. He and his family had served HIAS since its founding, and among his first acts as president was a tour of Europe's DP camps where 'hard case' Jews lingered, unable to emigrate. On his return, in his Rosh Hashana New Year's report on HIAS's achievements since the war—167,490 Jews had been helped to emigrate to Israel, the United States, and other countries—he cautioned the use of 'numbers' with these words:

> *Statistics are cold things, and one must look for the human story behind each figure. Each figure stands for the suffering of a human being. Each figure stands for the transplantation of a human soul, a Jewish soul, from wretchedness and terror to a good land and a good life.*

NOTES & REFERENCES

PAGE xii. Hebrew Immigrant Aid Society (HIAS) was incorporated in 1902, merging with and succeeding several immigration aid societies that went back to 1870 (Hebrew Emigrant Aid Society of the United States). For the organizational background and history of HIAS, see Mark Wischnitzer, *Visas to Freedom: The History of HIAS* (Cleveland, 1956). For other details of HIAS and of my family's connections to it, see notes to pages 72 and 73, below.

The term *She'erith Hapletah*, which appears throughout the Hebrew text of the Haggadah, will be translated, depending on the context, as 'survivors,' or 'the surviving remnants,' or the 'Saved Remnant,' or 'remnants.' Yehuda Bauer, the leading historian of the period, in his "The Initial Organization of the Holocaust Survivors in Bavaria," *Yad Vashem Studies on the European Jewish Catastrophe and Resistance* (Jerusalem, 1970), VIII, p. 127, explicates this term as follows: "We were unable to ascertain how the ancient Biblical term *She'erith Hapletah* ('the rest . . . that were escaped') . . . came to be applied to the survivors of the concentration camps in Germany. The phrase does not appear in any document in Germany before 20.7.1945, the date on which the [first] lists compiled by Rabbi Klausner were published." As can be seen from the title of his article, Bauer himself translates the term in this context as 'Holocaust survivors.' One will often see other transliterations of the Hebrew term, such as in the spelling of the titles to the volumes of Klausner's survivor lists, *Sharit Ha-Platah*. In the Haggadah here reproduced, the term is meant to include not only survivors of the camps, but Jews everywhere under Nazi rule who came out of the caves and forests, or from slave-labor sites, or from hiding elsewhere. For histories of the DP period, see next note.

PAGE xiii. For the DP period and the earliest history of Jewish survivors and their organization, see Leo W. Schwarz, *The Redeemers: A Saga of the Years 1945–1952* (New York, 1953). For the most authoritative, detailed, and comprehensive telling, see the works of Yehuda Bauer, *Out of the Ashes: The Impact of American Jews on Post-Holocaust European Jewry* (Oxford & New York, 1989); *Flight and Rescue: BRICHAH* (New York, 1970); and "The Initial Organization of the Holocaust Survivors in Bavaria," *Yad Vashem Studies*, cited above. See also Leonard Dinnerstein, *America and the Survivors of the Holocaust* (New York, 1982); Mark Wyman, *DP: Europe's Displaced Persons 1945–1951* (Philadelphia, 1989); Judah Nadich, *Eisenhower and the Jews* (New York, 1953); Alex Grobman, *Rekindling the Flame: American Jewish Chaplains and the Survivors of European Jewry, 1944–1948* (Detroit, 1993); and *Among the Survivors of the Holocaust—1945: The Landsberg DP Camp Letters of Major Irving Heymount, United States Army* (Cincinnati, 1982).

PAGE xv. The Dinnerstein book, cited above, contains the complete Harrison Commission Report. The quoted sentence is at pages 300–01. Among the Report's detailed descriptions of inadequate food and serious lack of needed medical supplies, the conditions of Jewish survivors in Germany and Austria are described as follows: "Generally speaking, three months after V-E Day and even longer after the liberation of individual groups, many Jewish displaced persons and other possible non-repatriables are living under guard behind barbed-wire fences, in camps of several descriptions (built by the Germans for slave-laborers and Jews) including some of the most notorious of the concentration camps, amidst crowded, frequently unsanitary and generally grim conditions, in complete idleness, with no opportunity, except surreptitiously, to communicate with the outside world, waiting, hoping for some word of encouragement and action on their behalf" (p. 292). For the calories count, and a good overall summary with statistics concerning the period 1945–1947, see the article "Displaced Persons" by Rabbi Philip S. Bernstein who, like Rabbi Judah Nadich, served as special advisor on Jewish affairs to the SHEAF Theater Commander (General McNarney who succeeded Eisenhower), in *American Jewish Yearbook* (1947), Vol. 49, pp. 520–33, esp. 523.

PAGE xvi. For the firing of Patton and his replacement by Truscott, see notes to page 11 below. For a history of the *Brichah*, see Bauer, *Flight and Rescue*, cited above.

PAGE xvii. Materials and accounts regarding Klausner's activities may be found in the published sources already noted; otherwise, they came from the editor's correspondence and interviews with Klausner conducted in 1997–1998, reports of which will be filed at YIVO Institute for Jewish Reasearch in New York City. A brief biography: Born Memphis, Tenn., 1915; educated in Denver schools through master's degree in 1938; entered the Hebrew Union College and was ordained in 1943. After serving as a rabbi to a New Haven congregation, he served as chaplain in the U.S. Army, during which time (1944–1948) he did the extraordinary work on behalf of the *She'erith Hapletah* that made him famous. Upon his return from the army he took up the cause of Jewish DPs by campaigning for the United Jewish Appeal. A career as rabbi of various congregations, educator, teacher, and editor followed, including the authorship of *The Bicentennial Passover Haggadah* (1976), a modernized traditional Haggadah with additions relating to Jewish Americana from the colonies to the present. He now lives in retirement in Santa Fe, New Mexico.

PAGE xviii. For the organization and function of the Central Committee, see Bauer, in *Yad Vashem Studies*, cited above; Klausner's words at page 149.

PAGE xix. Grobman, cited above, at page 121. Another version of this story appears in Klausner's preface to Volume I, Revised, of the *Sharit Ha-Platah* (Munich, 1946), where he writes that *Unzer Weg* "began with an old case of type found in a printing shop. From that case new letters were made." For a more detailed description of the discovery of the type and the founding of *Unzer Weg*, see Schwarz, *The Redeemers*, cited above, at pages

57–59. Since the printing/publishing activities of Stempel (*D. Stempel Schriftgiesserei A. G.*) included a type foundry, it is possible that the "case of type" (or the matrices) was discovered at the foundry. For the words about Klausner, see Grobman, cited above, page 130.

PAGE xx. For the words about 'organizing': Frank Stiffel, *The Tale of the Ring: A Kaddish (A personal memoir of The Holocaust)* (Wainscott, N.Y., 1984), p. 175.

PAGE xxi. For the quotation from Leo Schwarz, see *The Redeemers*, cited above, at page 61. The *Unzer Weg* issues are on microfilm, available at YIVO.

PAGE xxii. This dialogue appears in the Haggadah text on pages 33–35. Bitter factionalism was also the subject of Jewish humor, perennial even in the direst circumstances. See, for example, a broadside that offered satiric definitions, among them: "*Politics:* A permit for you to do what is forbidden to others. . . . *Member of the She'erith Hapletah:* A person whom three Jews organize; four inform, six agitate; and all make collections while he starves to death." From Schwarz, *The Redeemers*, cited above, at page 297.

PAGE xxiii. The *New York Times* materials on this and the next page are from Section 4, pages E1, 2, 12. The paper gives a lot of attention to the world's food shortages and hunger (cf. the article, "This is the Hunger that We Must Fight," by Albert Mayer, magazine section, p. 12 et seq.) and continues the next day (April 15) with a strong editorial and news items on the subject, including a report on that evening's Passover celebration, worldwide, and the need for aid for the survivors, noting that the baking of matzah in Germany for the first time in ten years had begun. Next to this last item is one headlined: "SEIZURES LIFT COSTS IN SMUGGLING JEWS: British Seen Bent on Making Price of Illegal Traffic to Palestine Prohibitive," page 5.

PAGE xxiv. For estimates of the number of Jews in Munich outside of camps in April 1946, see notes to page 7, below.

PAGE xxv. Quotation from Yaari at page x. For details of Haggadah bibliographies, see Appendix. *Nocham,* an acronym for *Noar Halutzi Meuhad,* in Hebrew means "consolation."

PAGE xxvi. Details of the life of Yosef Dov (Ber) Sheinson (b. Anyshkt, Kovno Province, Lithuania 1907, d. Canada 1990) may be found in three directories: Eli Gottesman, *Who's Who in Canadian Jewry* (1965); *100 Years of Yiddish and Hebrew Literature in Canada* [in Yiddish] ed. Charles L. Fox (Montreal, 1979); and *Leksikon fun Yiddish Shraybers*, ed. Berl Kagan (Brooklyn, 1986). These directory entries are, however, inconsistent with each other, though the Gottesman seems reliable. The main sources for the details presented here on Sheinson and on the first publication of the Haggadah are from correspondence and interviews with Y. D. Sheinson's widow, Mrs. Liza Sheinson of Montreal, and with Shlomo Shafir (originally Frenkel) now of Ramat Hasharon, Israel. Shafir (b. 1924) a historian, editor, and journalist, had been a student of Sheinson's and then a friend in Dachau-Kaufering slave-labor camp and in Munich 1945–1948 after liberation. He was active in *Achida* and editor of *Nitzotz* and *Dos Wort*, to which Sheinson contributed. In 1948 Shafir emigrated to Israel where, since 1974, he has been editor of the Hebrew journal *Gesher*. In 1948, Sheinson emigrated to Canada where, in Montreal, he continued with a distinguished career, internationally recognized, in Hebrew education until his death in 1990. The above source materials will be filed at YIVO.

Details of the Siauliai ghetto can be found in the *Encyclopedia of the Holocaust* (New York/London, 1990) entry: ŠIAULIAI (Shavli) .

PAGE xxviii. Berl Katznelson (b. Russia 1887, d. Palestine 1944) was a central figure in the Second Aliyah, a leader of the Labor Zionist movement, educator, and writer. He exercised a tremendous influence on the political ideas on which the State of Israel was eventually founded. David Frischmann (1859–1922) a Pole, was a major writer in modern Hebrew, writing poems, short stories, essays and criticism and editing several journals.

PAGE xxix. The *Jerusalem Post* article was in its *Magazine* of April 18, 1986 (David Geffen, "Free From Bondage"), page 4.

PAGE xxx. The Yad Vashem researcher is Tirza Oren, and the collector of Haggadot is Aviram Paz of Kibbutz Mishmar Ha'emek, Israel.

The sources of the story of the fate of the Debrecen Jews and the saving of a few were: Bauer, *Out of the Ashes*, cited above, page 11; *The Encyclopedia of the Holocaust* (New York / London, 1990) entries: DEBRECEN, A. EICHMANN, HUNGARY, R. KASZTNER, RELIEF AND RESCUE COMMITTEE OF BUDAPEST, STRASSHOF (a concentration camp near Vienna), and VIENNA. The '30,000 on ice' quotation is from the STRASSHOF entry (p. 1414). The HUNGARY entry details the story but puts the figure at 21,000. It describes how, between May 15 and July 9, 1944, the more than 430,000 Jews from the "countryside," which included Debrecen, were deported to death camps "in 147 trains composed of hermetically sealed freight cars. . . . A few transports, with about 21,000 Jews from the Southern part of Hungary, were directed to Strasshof, near Vienna, to be 'put on ice' pending the outcome of Zionist-SS negotiations" (p. 702). The RELIEF AND RESCUE entry states that among these 21,000 saved were a group from Debrecen (p. 1252).

A more detailed account of Miklós Adler's life follows: He was born in 1909 in a village known as Hajdúsamson, Hungary, and had a traditional Jewish upbringing and Hebrew education. Identified while young as talented in art, he was educated and trained as an artist and began teaching art at the Jewish high school in Debrecen while at the same time (1934–1944) he exhibited paintings and did woodcuts on biblical and literary themes. Transported by the Nazis in the spring of 1944, he survived as described in the text and returned to Debrecen in 1945 where he resumed teaching art. The *16 Fametszete* described in the Introduction was then printed at the Lieberman-Pannonia printing house in Debrecen. (The portfolio envelope also contained a note that the publication was done with the help of EZRA, a JDC-supported relief and rescue organization operating in Hungary.) Adler emigrated to Israel in 1957, lived in Holon, and died there in 1965 from injuries he had suffered from the beating in 1944. In Israel he used as his first name "Zvi."

The sources of information on Adler were communications with Mrs. Eva Adler Klein of London (Adler's sister); Gabor Katz of Staten Island, N.Y. (his nephew); Mrs. Irene Katz of Brooklyn, N.Y. (his sister-in-law)—

all of whom were on the same transport to Vienna—and Yoel Horovitz of Holon, Israel (a friend and former student of Adler's in Debrecen and Holon). Records of these communications will be filed at YIVO.

PAGE xxxi. In two of the Haggadah woodcuts, Sheinson might have discerned a double *beth* as the artist's mark, confirming to him that the only named artist was 'Ben Benyamin.' See in the upper right of the woodcut on page 20, and in the lower right of the woodcut on page 26.

The irony I observed continued among Adler's surviving family and friends who are mentioned in the preceding note. They did not know of the use of his woodcuts in the Sheinson Haggadah until my inquiries reached them through Tirza Oren at Yad Vashem as I prepared this edition in the summer of 1998. Once the connection was made between the 'Ben Benyamin' of the Haggadah and Miklós Adler, the Yad Vashem researchers could easily find their own holding of the *16 Fametszete*. An earlier citation of the *16 Fametszete*, noting the two names as belonging to the same artist, could be traced to Mendel Piekas, *The Holocaust and its Aftermath: Hebrew Books Published in the Years 1933–1972* [in Hebrew] (Jerusalem, 1974), II, p. 716.

PAGE xxxii. Adler's preface appeared in the four languages. The English, however, was a poor translation of the Hungarian/Hebrew. Therefore I worked up from translations of the other three the English version that is used here. In a similar way, I fashioned the English versions of Adler's woodcut titles that appear in the text.

PAGE 2. The "Munich Enclave" phrase was not an official designation; merely intending the Munich area.

PAGE 3. The story of the program to develop army print facilities, and the quotations, are from David Davidson, "Looking for the Good Germans," *American Heritage*, Vol. 33, June/July 1982, pp. 92–93. Michael Brenner in *After the Holocaust* (Princeton, 1997) describes the transformation of Yiddish periodicals within the DP camps when Hebrew type was first introduced (pp. 19–22). See also Gerd Korman, "Survivors' Talmud and the U.S. Army," *American Jewish History* 83 (March 1984), pp. 252–85.

This important study, too little known, tells the story of what was a monumental task. The U.S. Army, in cooperation with JDC and rabbinical authorities, printed the Talmud in nineteen volumes in 1948–1949 (Heidelberg, under supervision of Procurement Division, European Quartermaster Depot, U.S. Army). The border design of the title pages of this Talmud ascends from emblems of the Holocaust to a palm-leafed shore and then to a radiant Jerusalem, the Promised Land—thematically very much like several of Sheinson's designs. That edition was dedicated by the rabbinical authorities to the U.S. Army.

PAGE 5. In Yosef Hayim Yerushalmi's distinguished book *Haggadah and History* (Philadelphia, 1975), he observes how the Haggadah changed over time in both text and illustration to reflect contemporary events, especially those that affected Jewish survival. His many illustrations graphically demonstrate this point. As for Holocaust-related Haggadot, see pages 79–83, and for his treatment of a Haggadah that used the Sheinson Haggadah printing plates in 1948, see the Appendix to the present volume.

PAGE 7. The army's postwar 1945 estimates of 2,000 Jews living in Munich, and of 4,000–5,000 Jews "in all the cities of Bavaria," appear in Nadich, cited above, at page 152. The *Unzer Weg* estimate is from its April 15, 1946, issue; and the JDC gave its estimate in its Munich office report dated April 30, 1946, page 4. This last item can be found in JDC archives held at YIVO: LWSP, Folder 201, microfilm # 0385.

PAGE 8. The abbreviations are: CIC = Counter Intelligence Corps of the Army; CID = Central Intelligence Division; ICD = Information Control Division of the District Information Service's Control Command of Military Government; UNRRA = United Nations Relief and Rehabilitation Agency. The full name of the aid agency is the American Jewish Joint Distribution Committee; it is sometimes abbreviated into JDC, or AJDC, or simply and most commonly in Yiddish as "der Joint."

PAGE 9. The Truscott quotation is from Earl F. Ziemke, *The U.S. Army in the Occupation of Germany, 1944–1946* (Army Historical Series, Washington,

D.C., 1975). For use of the word "holocaust," see Jonathan Petrie, "'Holocaust' Had Its Uses Long Before the Second World War," a note in *Martyrdom and Resistance* 24, no. 3 (January–February 1998), p. 4.

The DP camps dwindled after 1948 until final closure in February 1957. For details, see notes to page 73 below.

PAGE 11. The Patton diary entries are dated September 15 and 17, 1945, in Martin Blumenson, *The Patton Papers, 1940–1945* (Boston, 1974), pp. 751, 753–54. The Truscott passage is from Lucian K. Truscott, *Command Missions: A Personal Story* (New York, 1954), p. 516.

Just before Truscott took command on October 7, 1945, Eisenhower gave him policy instructions. In Truscott's words, Eisenhower "repeated that the most acute and important problems with which we had to deal in Germany at that time were those involving denazification and the handling of . . . the victims of Nazi persecution. . . . We were to adopt a stern course with the Nazis. . . . also, he had prescribed preferential treatment for the Jewish displaced persons in the allowances of food, clothing, housing, and supplies, and had directed that no restrictions whatever were to be placed upon them." Truscott, cited above, at page 508.

The character of the quoted Patton entries on Jews and DPs could not be attributed solely to a particularly tense encounter with Eisenhower on their visit to a DP camp. In a number of other anti-Semitic entries, Patton reflects so deep and vitriolic a racism that a biographer, in no way unsympathetic, entitled one of his chapters "The Specter of Streicher," characterizing Patton's use of "the vocabulary of the defunct *Der Sturmer*, the Nazi newspaper in which Julius Streicher published his anti-Semitic diatribes." Ladislas Farago, *The Last Days of Patton* (New York, 1981), pp. 129, 137. Despite Patton's frequent comments on Jewish or 'non-Aryan' conspiracies against him, he has received a surprisingly fair-minded and thorough treatment at the hands of biographers and historians, Jewish as well as non-Jewish. Still, on these issues, Patton is a complex figure, as Farago's work makes clear. Farago notes "the considerable number of Jews on [Patton's] staff," and remarks on the choices of Patton and his family concerning the handling of his private papers. "Major Martin Blumenson, the Third Army historian, was also Jewish, hand-picked by Patton when others, fearful of Patton's alleged anti-Semitism, tried to get another detail for Blumenson. He was chosen by the family in 1966 and 1968 to publish Patton's outspoken papers, after decades of suppression following his death" (p. 100). In addition, there is a thorough and sympathetic treatment of Patton by the distinguished military historian, Carlo D'Este, in his recent *Patton: A Genius for War* (New York, 1995).

PAGE 15. The *Haroset* is traditionally made with chopped fruits, nuts, and matzah meal, laced with wine (suggesting the Jewish blood spilled by the Egyptians) and sweet spices, into a mortarlike consistency, reminiscent of the slaves' brickmaking in Egypt.

PAGE 17. For the 'two dishes,' see *The Passover Haggadah*, third revised edition, edited by Nahum N. Glatzer (New York, 1979), p. 8. The survivor is Solly Ganor, author of *Light One Candle: A Survivor's Tale from Lithuania to Jerusalem* (New York, 1995); in a personal communication.

PAGE 19. For question mark, see Menucha Gilboa, *Lexicon of Hebrew Periodicals in the 18th and 19th Centuries* [in Hebrew] (Jerusalem, 1992).

PAGE 21. Celan's poem is translated by John Felstiner in his *Paul Celan: Poet, Survivor, Jew* (New Haven, 1995), pp. 149–51.

PAGE 27. "One Year in Treblinka" from *The Death Camp Treblinka: A Documentary*, edited by Alexander Donat (The Holocaust Library, 1979); reprinted in *Art from the Ashes: A Holocaust Anthology*, ed. Lawrence L. Langer (New York, 1995), p.18.

PAGE 28. This was the misplaced page, here restored to proper sequence, as noted above on page 1 and in the Appendix at II.

PAGE 35. For rabbinic quotation, see Glatzer, cited above, page 21, footnote.

PAGE 39. From *Collected Poems*, translated by Ruth Feldman and Brian Swann (London/Boston, 1988).

PAGE 43. From Stiffel, *A Tale of the Ring*, chapter 9, especially pages 189–202.

PAGE 47. For vernacular, see Glatzer, cited above, page 23, footnote.

PAGE 55. From Report of U.S. Army, Seventy-first Infantry Division, *The*

Seventy-First Came to Gunskirchen Lager (Augsburg, Germany, 1945), foreword by the commanding officer, Maj. Gen. Willard G. Wyman. The quoted passage is from a report of Capt. J. D. Pletcher, Seventy-first Division Headquarters, pages 9–10. Gunskirchen was an assembly camp for Jewish prisoners from Mauthausen concentration camp, begun late in the war. Radnóti's poem is dated September 1944 and can be found in *Foamy Sky: The Major Poems of Miklós Radnóti,* selected and translated by Zsuzsuanna Ozsváth and Frederick Turner (Princeton, 1992); reprinted in Langer, notes to page 27 above, at page 232.

PAGE 61. Levi's words are from *Survival at Auschwitz: The Nazi Assault on Humanity* [orig. 1958] (Touchstone Edition, 1996), page 20. The Pagis poem is translated by John Felstiner and printed with his permission.

PAGE 65. *Out of the Ashes,* cited above, at pages 294–96.

PAGE 67. The German-Jewish poet Nelly Sachs was, through the intervention of the Swedish Nobel-laureate novelist Selma Lagerlof, permitted to emigrate to Sweden in 1940. There she wrote a powerful poetry about the Holocaust that earned her a Nobel Prize for Literature in 1966. One of her volumes is titled *O the Chimneys.* The Glatstein lines are from *Cloud-Jew* and *Smoke* in *Selected Poems of Yankev Glatshteyn,* edited and translated by Richard J. Fein (Philadelphia, 1987); reprinted in Langer, notes to page 27 above, at pages 660–61.

PAGE 72. Joseph Levine (b. Russia, 1907; d. Fort Wayne, Indiana, 1996). During World War I, his family was driven from home by German incursions and made its way east to Manchuria and eventually to the United States where he was educated and became a social worker. At the conclusion of World War II, he served with JDC/UNRRA in 1945–1946, posted in Schwandorff and then Regensburg in eastern Bavaria; but he often worked with Klausner out of the JDC's main office in Munich about 120 km. away. It was probably at Klausner's second-night Seder that Levine acquired copies of the "A" Haggadah; in addition to the one given to my parents, there was a copy he retained that, according to his family, he cherished and showed frequently. After returning to the United States he became in 1947 executive director of the Fort Wayne Jewish Federation. He retired in 1972 to become executive director of the Indiana Jewish Historical Society from which he retired in 1992. He was interviewed and appeared in Studs Terkel's *"The Good War": An Oral History of World War Two* (New York, 1984), pp. 437–43. When or where this inscription of the "A" Haggadah was made to my parents has not been determined.

PAGE 73. As I have assumed that this inscription was made to my parents as representatives of HIAS, I should like to honor in this note my family's long connections with this organization. My father, Ben Touster (1893–1979), was for many years a HIAS board member and served as its president from 1952 to 1956. After presiding over the consolidation of Jewish immigration services into United HIAS Services, he devoted much of his time to CARE, where he served as treasurer, vice-president, and then chairman of the board. My mother, Bertha [Landau] Touster (1895–1973), long active in many charities, served HIAS as a leader in the women's division and later as a board member. Eldest and most beloved was my uncle, John L. Bernstein (1873–1952), who was a founder and the first vice-president of HIAS at its incorporation in 1902. He then became president in 1917 and led HIAS in helping the large number of European refugees during post-World War I, stepping down in 1926. But he remained throughout his life a guiding spirit for rescue and immigration among Jews throughout the world, aided always by his wife, Celia [Richter] Bernstein (1881–1944). She, a wonderful woman, not only served long in the HIAS Women's Division, but presided over a large warm home that became an extraordinary salon during the thirties, where refugee artists, writers, and intellectuals gathered. John L.'s younger brother, my uncle Dr. James Bernstein (1875–1959), gave up a medical practice to become the HIAS representative and then director of European operations, serving in the twenties in Warsaw and Berlin, in the thirties in Paris, and then in Lisbon during the war years. His wife, my aunt Anna [Touster] Bernstein (1881–1971), served with him as a model diplomat's wife at each posted city. My cousin Dr. Florence [Bernstein] Freedman (1908–1995), a professor of English at Hunter College, became for a time head of the HIAS Women's Division, as did my cousin Bertha [Jarvis] Benton (1908–1991). My cousin Edward M. Benton (1906–1988), an attorney, served as board member from the thirties and became its general counsel. It was in his office that I served as assistant counsel in the early fifties. In retrospect, I see cousins and 'cousins' everywhere doing things for HIAS in the reception and care of immigrants, as if the whole family had been chosen for a vocation.

My parents' tour of the European DP camps was reported in the May 23, 1952, edition of the *New York Times*. My father's report, dated September 18, 1952, is available in the HIAS archives.

APPENDIX

Notes on the bibliography of Haggadot and the place of the "A" Haggadah.

****

I. There are two modern comprehensive Haggadah bibliographies, both of which cite the "A" Haggadah. They are:

1. Abraham Yaari, *Bibliography of the Passover Haggadah from the Earliest Printed Edition to 1960* [in Hebrew] (Jerusalem, 1960). Item # 2328, page 162. Following its description of the Haggadah, the entry contains only this parenthetical reference to what was, presumably, a mention or discussion of the Haggadah: "(Musée d'Art Juif, Paris. Pessah dans l'art folklorique Juif, Paris 1951, p. 8, no. 76)." The piece referred to was not available at the Musée which is presently relocating and reorganizing to become the Musée d'Art et d'Histoire du Judaisme. The librarian believes the piece cited is from a museum catalogue but is uncertain as to whether it will be found in the archives. Despite efforts made through other sources, I have been unable to find the text at any library.

2. Isaac Yudlov, *The Haggadah Thesaurus Bibliography of Passover Haggadot from the Beginning of Hebrew Printing until 1960* [in Hebrew] (Jerusalem, 1997). Item #4007, page 293, referring to the above Yaari citation.

II. Neither of the bibliographies has a separate entry for the Sheinson Haggadah that preceded, probably by a few weeks, the printing of the "A"

Haggadah which, as described in the Introduction, used the thirty Sheinson photo-engraved printing plates and added to it four pages. These added pages had English text placed within the frame of Sheinson's formatted margin designs, thus utilizing the existing printing plates. They were the English title page, two pages of Klausner's preface, and an epigraph page in English ["We were slaves to Hitler in Germany . . ."] within a *Brause Bad* format. The only other difference in the reprinting was that four pages of Yiddish passages were moved toward the end of the book, thus causing two of the woodcuts to change their placement and one of the pages of the Hebrew text to be placed out of context (which is corrected in this edition).

III. In addition to the Yaari and Yudlov bibliographies noted above, there is another major modern work on Haggadah scholarship: Yosef Hayim Yerushalmi, *Haggadah and History: A Panorama in Facsimile of Five Centuries of the Printed Haggadah from the Collections of Harvard University and the Jewish Theological Seminary in America* (Philadelphia, 1975). In this book, depending as it does on two particular collections, neither the Sheinson nor the "A" Haggadah is cited. But there is a reference to a Haggadah from Munich dated 1948, published by Noar Halutzi Meuhad (*Nocham*), with facsimile pages appearing as Plates #178–181. The last three plates turn out to be reproductions of three pages from the Sheinson Haggadah that had appeared two years before. This *Nocham* Haggadah which I examined at the Harvard Judaica Collection is clearly another edition of Sheinson's Haggadah with some important changes. It has a new front cover/title page identifying itself not as a 'supplement,' but simply "Haggadah for Passover" and naming *Nocham* as the sole publisher. It was apparently (on the basis of style) designed by Sheinson. Other changes were: it had neither the Order of the Seder page, nor the colophon page identifying *Achida* as copublisher or Sheinson as arranger and illustrator; and it had a new back cover in Hebrew bold letters stating "Pesach 5708 Munich." It contains only two 'Ben Benyamin' woodcuts out of the seven in the original, and there are seventeen pages of text as against twenty-one in the original. Within the frame of the same Sheinson plates of formatted border designs, text variations were made—many minor, but some major, such as the inclusion of Bialik poetry on four pages.

IV. In 1987–1988, John Najmann of London (who survived the Holocaust as a fourteen-year-old on the *Kindertransport* from Germany to England in December 1938) had printed by means of photocopy several hundred copies of the "A" Haggadah; and in 1993–1994, a few hundred more. Reproduced in black and white by Xerox (probably by Kall Kwik of Golders Green, London), these copies were distributed by Najmann to friends and Holocaust-related institutions, in the United Kingdom, Israel, and Europe. At the same time he gave his original copy to Yad Vashem. He was a witness to events in and around Munich during the postwar months, 1945–1946, as a civilian employee of the military government. It was Klausner who helped him find his mother, a survivor of Auschwitz. Najmann attended one of the Klausner Seders, where he acquired his "A" Haggadah. He provided his own unpublished translation of it to this editor during the summer of 1998, the week of his sudden death while at Yad Vashem, where he and his wife Hertha had gone to establish a memorial fund honoring his parents.

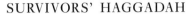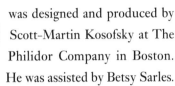SURVIVORS' HAGGADAH was designed and produced by Scott-Martin Kosofsky at The Philidor Company in Boston. He was assisted by Betsy Sarles. Marlowe Bergendoff was the copy editor. The introduction, notes, and commentaries were set in Philidor Erhardt, a family of typefaces made by Mr. Kosofsky in 1996, patterned after the "real Dutch types" offered by the Erhardt foundry in Leipzig in the mid-eighteenth century. The translations were set in Erik Spiekermann's 1991 Meta types, a family of humanistic sans-serif typefaces that are outstanding for their readability. Matthew Carter's Mantinia was used for the titles.

The book was created on a Macintosh computer. Mr. Kosofsky scanned the original Haggadah at Aurora Graphics, Portsmouth, New Hampshire. Mercantile Printing of Worcester, Massachusetts, printed the book; it was bound by Acme Bookbinding of Charlestown, Massachusetts. The barbed-wire pattern on the binding was derived from a photograph by Sophie Kosofsky.